Blessed Are You

D1409235

Blessed Are You

THE BEATITUDES AND OUR SURVIVAL

Evelyn Mattern

Foreword by
MICHAEL H. CROSBY

Evelyn Mattern, S.F.C.C. is a Sister for Christian Community. She has been involved in teaching, peace and justice ministry, and ecumenical affairs for over twenty years and is currently Instructor of English at Wake Tech Community College in North Carolina. Her articles and poetry have been published in *America, Commonweal, Sojourners, Christian Century,* and *National Catholic Reporter.*

Unless otherwise noted, the scripture quotations are from *The New English Bible,* copyright © 1970, Oxford University Press and Cambridge University Press.

International Standard Book Number: 0-87793-534-3

Library of Congress Catalog Card Number: 94-71728

Cover and text design by Katherine Robinson Coleman

Cover photograph by Vernon Sigl

Photography: Philip Gendreau 68; Vernon Sigl 14, 100; Justin Soleta 8, 26, 38, 56, 116, 134.

Printed and bound in the United States of America.

For my friend Mary Chupein, S.F.C.C.,
who lived them

Contents

ℱoreword

For more than fifteen years, I have taught a course on the beatitudes in Matthew's gospel at Retreats International at the University of Notre Dame. The participants tend to be people involved full-time in church ministry. There are priests and ministers, women and men religious, and lay professionals.

At the opening session I have often asked the class to write down or verbally share with the group the eight beatitudes of Matthew. I say: "You don't need to have them in order, but you can't have the first part of one joined by the last part of another, like 'Blessed are the poor in spirit, they will be satisfied.'" In return for any completed list I promise a free copy of any one of my books.

At this point their mental confusion begins to appear in their body language. It's clear that they don't know, and what's embarrassing for them becomes a teachable moment for me. On average I've been giving away one book for every forty-two participants. The last time I asked my students to give me their lists, over eighty were in attendance. Only one person, a Mennonite pastor, was able to list all eight beatitudes—and he did so in proper order as well!

Why is it that in such a large group of people only one or two might know the eight beatitudes, while only one or two would *not* know the ten commandments? Is our moral life and discipleship still defined by the Mosaic code rather than the core teachings of Jesus? Recently I saw an advertisement for the Catholic school system in the Diocese of Dallas in the Sunday newspaper: "We teach by the numbers." The numbers were not one to eight around the beatitudes but one to ten around the commandments.

Even in his encyclical on the moral foundations of life, *Veritatis Splendor*, Pope John Paul II seems to define moral life more according to the commandments than the beatitudes. However, he does explain:

> There is no separation or opposition between the beatitudes and the commandments: both refer to the good, to eternal life. The Sermon on the Mount begins with the proclamation of the beatitudes, but also refers to the commandments (cf. Mt 5:20-48). At the same time, the Sermon on the Mount demonstrates the openness of the commandments and their orientation toward the horizon of the perfection proper to the beatitudes (n. 16, *Origins* 23, 1993).

Many writers, including myself, believe that the main body of Matthew's gospel is divided into five books and that the summary of all the books is in the first teaching, the Sermon on the Mount. We also note that the Sermon on the Mount can be summarized in its first teachings, the beatitudes. I also believe that the first beatitude, "Blessed are the poor in spirit, the reign of God is theirs," serves as a summary statement of the beatitudes and, thus, of the whole teaching of Jesus.

If the beatitudes are so central to Jesus' message in Matthew's gospel, we can rightly ask why such little heed is given them. Some writers explain that we don't need to pay much attention to the beatitudes because they are merely exhortative; they have no moral necessity. Others say they only apply to people at certain levels of the spiritual life. Still others dismiss them as attitudes for another age rather than action-orientations for our own. In a similar vein, some argue that the New Testament beatitudes do not speak to our contemporary era because it has developed its own set of beatitudes or the rewards that come to those who inherit the "good life."

One reason, I think, why the beatitudes have not been taken seriously as guidelines for discipleship is that few authors have applied them well to contemporary life. With *Blessed Are You* Evelyn Mattern should put an end to that objection. With example after example from her own and others' lives as well as her ability to draw on a host of writers from Simone Weil to Oscar Romero to Jose Ortega y Gasset, she invites the reader to accept them in the spirit that Matthew's Jesus offered them: as a challenge to contemporary people in our culture to take seriously Jesus' call to embrace his teachings as a way of life.

When I first learned about this book, it was still in its infancy. Frank Cunningham, the Director of Publishing for Ave Maria Press, asked me to read over an early draft to get my opinion on its merits for publication. I read the first draft with mild interest and said I thought it should be pursued. By the time I was presented with the final copy I had moved from general openness to enthusiastic support.

Here and there I have found myself quibbling with the author over a possible tendency to overlook distinctions in the Matthean and Lukan texts as well as her ability to move indiscriminately from one gospel to another, or from Matthew to Paul without adequate contextualization. I wanted her to stick with Matthew to appease my scriptural sensitivities. However, the more I read *her* text, the more I moved from my head to my heart, from academic concerns to concerns about my own spirituality, and to questions about how I am or am not translating the beatitudes into my life, my relationships, and my world.

While her exegesis might not always get to the context of the beatitudes as I might want, it gets to the heart of the beatitudes in a way that I need. Just as I would be arguing with her regarding some academic issue, I read something

that challenged me at my core which told me to keep quiet
and keep reading. Her text invited me to stop debating and
to start listening. In fact I found myself invariably disap-
pointed when I would come to the conclusion of each chap-
ter. I wanted more.

If the beatitudes were wisdom sayings for the first century, Evelyn Mattern's book is wisdom literature for our age.
For instance, in addressing "Blessed are the poor in spirit, for
theirs is the reign of God," she discusses shopping as
"America's salvation." She notes that our malls are looking
more and more "Like the contemporary equivalent of
medieval cathedrals, complete with holiday shrines and
lights directing the eye to icons for veneration." In showing
how they have captured our hearts and minds, she poignant-
ly notes:

> The malls are open when churches are closed. They
> are especially full around holidays like Christmas
> and Easter, which originated in the church's cycle
> of celebration but now anchor the annual spending
> cycle that makes the economy hum. Our economy
> is "saved" by Christmas and Easter, even as we are
> not. We have come to depend on our goods, not on
> our God.

The author's wisdom is not ethereal but realistic. Nor is
it apocalyptic. One might say it serves as a kind of apologia
or examination of conscience for each of us. For instance, in
discussing people like Mahatma Gandhi, Martin Luther
King, Jr. and Dorothy Day as models of meekness she sagely
writes:

> I mention these three public figures precisely be-
> cause they were not perfect. They were also not
> servile or passive. But they were meek. Despite
> personal weakness or fragility, they learned to
> respond appropriately to the structurally violent
> situations endemic to our time.

Evelyn Mattern's own wisdom appears in her many one-liners as well.

> Mourning brings to memory the dimension of the heart, and in the case of a society that has inflicted pain, the willingness to ask forgiveness and to change.

> Where supermarkets and microwave ovens abound, it is not easy to know hunger and thirst, let alone hunger and thirst for a seeming abstraction like justice.

> Prevention can be a form of repentance.

> Mercy ... does not distinguish between deserving and undeserving because in the eyes of God we are all both.

> Sometimes, mercy is the only justice.

Written from her position of privilege, the author has not been aloof from marginated people whether they be in her state of North Carolina or among the campesinos of Nicaragua. Such experiences help make the book's wisdom practical as well, as when we are told that peacemaking requires initiative, vulnerability, and imagination. In addition to such a triad, we are given examples of each that make the wisdom-message applicable to daily life and conflictual situations. Thus Mattern's wisdom is not home-spun; it is realistic and sound.

In one place the author speaks of Shakespeare's dying King Lear who begs his listeners to "tell my story and tell it right." She explains that "human beings long to be heard because true hearing constitutes understanding." It was not difficult at all to "listen" to Evelyn Mattern's story because she has told the beatitudes "story" right. In her interpretation I have understood better how I can live out these core teachings of Matthew's Jesus in our world today. I invite the faith-filled reader to "listen" to her as well!

Michael H. Crosby, O.F.M. Cap.

Introduction

When I was in the novitiate on the eve of Vatican II and learning to be a Roman Catholic sister, we did some scripture study and read numerous books on the history of religious life, on asceticism, and on "keeping the rule." I remember an entire series that was read aloud to us during silent meals: *The Rule in Other Words, The Vows in Other Words, Obedience in Other Words*. There must have been a dozen of those *In Other Words* books. They had in common a focus on the "laws" of religious living.

Only years later did I realize how much time we wasted with those books and with others like Tanqueray's manual of asceticism that divided and subdivided into hundreds of categories the stages of the ascetical and mystical life. I can still remember the aroma of the soft leather-bound volume I fell heir to and the feel of its fine, thin pages as I turned them in pursuit of discovering where I was on the mystical ladder, even as I read that one was not to indulge in speculation about such things.

Quite some time after Vatican II and the renewal courses in scripture study that were plentiful in its wake, I understood that the novitiate was a missed opportunity insofar as we spent more time reading "spiritual books" than we did studying scripture. By then I was teaching World Literature courses and found that the World Lit texts usually included the Book of Job to exemplify the writing of the Old Testament and the beatitudes to exemplify the New Testament. College students who knew nothing about Christianity were expected to comprehend it by reading that small section of the Sermon on the Mount. It was especially hard to teach the beatitudes to students from Christian backgrounds. Most of them had learned that the ten commandments were more important than the beatitudes and that Jesus probably didn't mean us to take the latter so seriously because they were so much harder to "pin down."

Nevertheless I credit those textbook editors with greater acuity than I did twenty years ago. Having lived more decades trying to be a Christian, struggling to understand and live the gospel, I see now that we would have better spent our novitiate years pondering the beatitudes because they are in a sense the essential gospel, the distillation of Jesus' teaching, and the plan for attitude and action that he laid out. And I wish my Christian students had had religious education courses that focused on the beatitudes.

The beatitudes, recorded by two of the four evangelists, are a traditional literary type, like parables, that Jesus adapted to his purposes. Dennis Hamm points out that in Luke 11:27-28 a woman in the crowd uses the conventional form to express her worldly wisdom, "Blessed is the womb that bore you and the breasts that nursed you." And Jesus responds within the tradition, "Rather blessed are they who hear the word of God and keep it." The very first psalm of the psalter says,

> Blessed is the [person] who walks not
> in the counsel of the wicked. ...
> [This person] is like a tree planted by streams of water,
> that yields its fruit in due season,
> and its leaf does not wither.

All three of these beatitudes promise that the good person will be happy.

Scholars usually distinguish between wisdom beatitudes and apocalyptic beatitudes, the former emphasizing attitudes and behavior valuable in the present moment, the latter stressing God's future rewards. Both kinds are also called *"Macarisms"* because the earliest translations use the Greek word *makarios,* which means "blessed" or "fortunate" or "happy." According to Hamm, most of the forty-four New Testament macarisms are apocalyptic beatitudes, but both types, whether highlighting the goods of "this age" or the "age to come," affirm a "blessed relationship with God in the present" (Hamm, p. 11).

Luke records four beatitudes and four corresponding woes for those who do not put on the recommended attitude. Matthew gives us nine beatitudes, the last one really an expansion of the eighth. Many commentators think Luke's rendition more concrete and hard-hitting in its message on behalf of the poor, but it is generally agreed that both writers used a common prior source for Jesus' sayings.

Raymond Collins sums up the view of many who find Matthew's version more transparent in its concern to spell out the gospel's implications for life. He thinks that some of Matthew's beatitudes are formulations of an earlier tradition, some his own creation.

> In the tradition, the beatitudes were originally an element of proclamation. They echoed Jesus' proclamation that the Reign of God is for the poor and other social outcasts. In Matthew's version ... proclamation has given way to catechesis. By adapting the traditional beatitudes and formulating additional ones, Matthew has catechetically spelled out the qualities of the disciple (Collins, p. 308).

In short, Luke proclaims, Matthew teaches.

Because of Matthew's emphasis on forming us to be disciples, I will discuss primarily the Matthean version of the beatitudes. Also, I choose the English translation "blessed" over "happy" because the latter word often signifies in our

culture a merely emotional state not necessarily rooted in
right relations with others and with God.

> Blessed are the poor in spirit, for theirs
> is the kingdom of heaven.
>
> Blessed are those who mourn, for they
> shall be comforted.
>
> Blessed are the meek, for they shall
> inherit the earth.
>
> Blessed are those who hunger and thirst
> for righteousness, for they shall be satisfied.
>
> Blessed are the merciful, for they shall
> obtain mercy.
>
> Blessed are the pure in heart, for they
> shall see God.
>
> Blessed are the peacemakers, for they
> shall be called sons of God.
>
> Blessed are those who are persecuted
> for righteousness' sake, for theirs
> is the kingdom of heaven.
>
> Blessed are you when they revile and
> persecute you and utter all kinds
> of evil against you falsely on my
> account. Rejoice and be glad for your reward
> is great in heaven, for so they
> persecuted the prophets who were
> before you (Mt 5:3-12, *RSV*).

Although all beatitudes promise that the good person
will be happy, Jesus' beatitudes in the Sermon on the
Mount—whether from Luke or Matthew—spell out in a
startling and untraditional way who the good person is.
Unlike the woman who blessed him according to the conven-

tional wisdom, "Blessed is the womb that bore you," Jesus blesses the losers of this world. The poor of whom he speaks are unlikely to be hallowed by the conventional wisdom of many cultures, ours in particular.

Poverty, meekness, mourning, and purity of heart are not values trumpeted by the mass media and are unlikely to guarantee their practitioners success. But in a world where more and more people seem to be losing, are roped out of the success loop and increasingly marginal to the political, economic, and cultural life of their societies, we may need more than ever a program for the underdog.

The beatitudes are a call to marginalize ourselves from our culture. Bishop Helder Camara, who worked many years with the poorest people in the northeast of Brazil, calls marginalization a universal phenomenon today:

> Anyone who has stood by the road trying to hitch a lift in a hurry and watched the motor cars flash past him, can understand what is meant by "marginal."

> A marginal person is someone who is left by the wayside in the economic, social, political and cultural life of his country.

> We could imagine that in an underdeveloped country the whole population would be living in the same subhuman conditions. But this is not the case. What usually happens might be called an internal colonialism. Small groups of rich people live off the poverty of their fellow citizens. ...

> We could imagine that there are no marginal persons in developed countries. This is also false. Even in rich countries there are groups who remain poor, remain marginal. ...

> Marginalization does not only affect groups or individuals. There exist today marginal countries or even continents. This is what we mean by the

"third world," Africa, Asia and Latin America
(Camara, p. 36).

The hungry, the homeless, the impoverished, refugees,
abused children, prisoners, addicts, elderly people discarded
in nursing homes, victims of war: add them all together and
you have a majority of the world's population. This mar-
ginalized majority reflects many of the characteristics of the
multitudes Jesus addressed. They were for the most part
poor, a downtrodden people, the "wretched of the earth"
colonized by Rome and betrayed by their own leaders. They
were, moreover, familiar from their scriptures with the "up-
side-down" nature of the world of God's justice invoked by
Mary in the Magnificat:

He has put down the mighty from their thrones,
and exalted those of low degree;
he has filled the hungry with good things,
and the rich he has sent empty away (Lk 1:52-53).

The beatitudes derive from a form of speech in wisdom
literature where common sense ideals are held up by the
speaker in order to show the listeners how to get ahead. In
Jesus' case, however, he states the joy or blessedness of those
who embody the less than ideal state of falling behind. And
he not only describes but also demonstrates in his life the
fruits attainable in these marginal situations where faith,
hope, and love remain possible, despite the loss of all else
that would seem to be necessary for human happiness.

Indeed, the beatitudes are the living out of the upside-
down values of faith, hope, and love. Faith, the impossibly
small mustard seed that gives birth to the improbably large
tree. Hope, trust over and against the facts, when despair
seems infinitely more logical. Love, the bearing of another's
yoke by one who feels she can hardly shoulder her own
without stumbling.

Although Jesus was a man of action and usually taught
through action, he also used parables, brief stories told in
response to specific questions and occasions. We might con-

sider the Sermon on the Mount with its beatitudes a summary or outline of his thinking, as though he said to himself
one bright morning looking out across the lapping waters of
the Sea of Galilee, "Just what is it I want to say? How shall I
sum it up?"

He begins significantly with a consideration of the end,
happiness or blessedness. He cares less about behavior than
the attitudes that generate it. What is it like to be the person
who acts that God's will be done on earth? What lives in the
heart of the one who does God's will? "Love God and do
what you will," says St. Augustine. What is the quality of the
love practiced by the one who, in Augustine's terms, can then
feel free to do what she wants?

The one who loves with such a love is the one who
experiences blessedness in the here and now. The consequences of that love, its broad outlines filled in by the
descriptions given in the beatitudes, are not reserved for
another time and place. Jesus does not promise an immediate, or eventual, paradise consisting of golden lounge chairs
and beautiful people feeding us caviar and champagne. But
makarios means "blessed" and was accompanied by the
present tense; that is, blessedness comes now to the one who
is poor or gentle or pure of heart. Rewards are not reserved
for the future. Hard as it is for most of us to credit, those who
have experienced the bliss of the beatitudes can affirm that it
comes in the present, even in the midst of hardship and
conflict. Even while bearing the cross.

Especially when we know we are bearing the cross can
we be joyful. French philosopher and mystic Simone Weil
cautions us not to use the word "cross" to describe our little
daily troubles. She considers it a near sacrilegious abuse of
language to refer to these as our crosses. She defines the cross
as "the whole of that necessity by which the infinity of space
and time is filled and which, in given circumstances, can be
concentrated upon the atom that any one of us is, and totally
pulverize it." Weil says that the person who truly, concretely,
and all the time, recognizes and accepts lovingly the

possibility of this affliction can experience happiness in the midst of it. And she adds we must embrace it closely "even if it offers its roughest surface and the roughness cuts into us" (Weil, *Reader*, p. 455).

We all occasionally see the joy of those who suffer extreme necessity or pain. Radiant on their deathbed or exquisitely concerned for the welfare of others in the midst of their own affliction, they elicit comments from friends who claim they are "getting the grace" to bear their sorrows or are living in the calm at the center of the storm. The phenomenon of the suffering one who is joyful cannot be dismissed. It is the reality that each of the beatitudes cites in the second half of its statement. The gift of the beatitude both accompanies and is a consequence of it. Blessed are the poor in spirit, for theirs is the kingdom. The kingdom both results from and accompanies the poverty. Blessed are the meek, for they shall possess. Because and while they are gentle, they shall have everything. Because they claim little, they shall have much. Above all, they shall know joy.

The beatitudes send a message vital to our times. Several years ago I stood on a hillside overlooking the Sea of Galilee, considered a likely site of the Sermon on the Mount. A fellow pilgrim asked, "Do you think the beatitudes are an impossible dream that we're merely to aspire toward, or are they somehow meant to be practiced in the everyday?" Perhaps because we had just passed through several military checkpoints manned by heavily armed soldiers that reminded us of how harsh and volatile life is in Israel/Palestine and many other parts of the world today, I responded with feeling, "They are meant to be lived, or else we perish." In that moment it was clear to me that if the beatitudes ever were merely a pious ideal meant to hallow a few, circumstances today require them as a practicable program to enable all of us to survive.

Scholars contrast the beatitudes with the law, which by its nature demands the minimum of us. "Keep the rule, and the rule will keep you," our sage novice mistress and many who had gone before her used to say. In other words, answer the bell, get needed permissions, and accept your superiors' decisions. In more worldly terms, don't exceed the limit, cheat on your taxes, or fool with your neighbor's wife. Jesus, on the other hand, because of his love for us, can ask the maximum. And he does so in the beatitudes, which demand more of us than our own egos or careful attention to legal detail could ever give.

The beatitudes are meant to be lived daily in this troubled world of ours, and some of the greatest seekers and lovers of humanity in our time have arrived by different paths at insights like them. Mahatma Gandhi's commitment to the path of loving, non-violent change was partially inspired by Jesus but also eked out of his own "experiments with truth" that showed him how only poverty of spirit and purity of heart could lead humanity away from the abyss we currently lurch above.

Similarly, Thich Nhat Hanh, a Vietnamese Buddhist monk and peacemaker, teaches a way of being that closely resembles the inner posture outlined by the beatitudes. He describes a life that will enable humanity and the earth to survive, a life of awareness and community with all living beings. Increasingly, thinkers grappling with the human surge toward self-destruction and despoliation of the earth are achieving insights similar to those informing the beatitudes. At least that part of the Christian message is hearable by seekers after solutions to intractable human problems. And since it is the core of the Christian message, our rediscovering it as Christians may let us show it forth more clearly and forcefully.

Christian practitioners of the beatitudes and proponents of non-violent action in the world have in common the understanding of faith, hope, and love described by Thomas Merton in his essay, "Blessed Are the Meek." Faith informs us that the kingdom of God has come, says Merton, and we can afford to "renounce the protection of violence and risk being humble, that is, *vulnerable*." Similarly, Christians and non-violent persons live in hope, unlike the millions in the world "secretly convinced that only tragedy and evil can result from our present situation." Above all, such Christians also love, refusing to despair of the world and abandon it to its evil fate.

Considering the beatitudes liveable may be the sign of the Christian and of anyone who seeks to help save our world today.

Whenever possible, I have used inclusive language. In some of the quotes used, however, it was not possible to change the text.

1

Blessed Are the Poor in Spirit

When I was in high school, a religion teacher told our class that the eye of the needle that the rich man's camel would have to pass through to get into the kingdom of heaven was really the hole in Cleopatra's needle, a giant obelisk erected by the pharaoh at Alexandria. I think of that eccentric illustration every time I hear a discussion in church or academic circles of whether Jesus blessed the materially poor or the poor in spirit. We, to whom hard sayings apply, resort to casuistry to deny that they mean what they say. Why else is it so difficult to accept that the materially poor are more likely to be poor in spirit?

The issue of spiritual vs. material poverty is a theoretical discussion conducted mostly by the non-poor. In Ernesto Cardenal's *The Gospel in Solentiname* several Nicaraguan campesinos talk about what it means to be poor in spirit and conclude that it means to love God and neighbor, but that is hard for the rich to do. One campesino, Oscar, says, "I believe that we need to be clear about this: you love either God or money. Don't you dedicate yourself to making money? For the one who loves money, that is his god. Another who loves God? That one shares his money and is poor. Then he is able to live in love" (Cardenal, vol. 1, p. 93).

A similar conclusion emerges in a book of dialogues between the Jesuit priest and poet Daniel Berrigan and the Vietnamese Buddhist monk Thich Nhat Hanh. "If you have compassion, you cannot be rich. ... But it seems that compassion, both in Buddhism and in Christianity, is so important, so basic, that you can be rich only when you can bear the sight of suffering. If you cannot bear that, you have to give your possessions away" (Berrigan and Hanh, p. 102). In the view of both Thich Nhat Hanh and the campesino Oscar, those who love God, whether they start out rich or poor, will soon become materially poor. Their compassion will prompt them to divest themselves of belongings they don't need.

The Greek word for "poor" used in the New Testament to translate the Aramaic *ani, anaw, ebion* is *ptochos*, meaning "one for whom something necessary for survival is lacking." It literally means "to squat," to be bent over and suppliant, and differs from the Greek *penes*, which denotes "working man," one who can provide for himself. The lives of the poor, *ptochos*, are economically intolerable. The poor totally lack resources to provide for their own needs. They could be beggars in first century Palestine or homeless people today.

In traditional Jewish piety, poverty and utter dependence on God are synonymous. To have to depend entirely on God alerts one to the presence of God. Without God, all else absent, one simply does not survive. The poor survive believing that, if they owned a camel, God would have bestowed it on them and could guide it through the eye of even the seamstress' needle.

Most of us have known some poverty in our lives, days or months or years when we lived from moment to moment; perhaps we didn't know where our children's next meal would come from, or we sensed a friend was in great physical or moral danger, or we accompanied a loved one in the last stages of dying. Whatever the cause, we were unable to look beyond the instant and felt ourselves upheld in each moment, aware of the war between numbness and raw wounds at the edge of consciousness. That is poverty of spirit, dependence on God alone.

Such dependence can open us to God's presence in our lives. An agnostic woman I know recently endured the death of her two-year-old child. In her agony she felt absurdity slice through the dailiness, the normalcy of her middle class American life. Suddenly she no longer noticed the presence or absence of things that had previously meant much to her. Months later she mused that her daughter's death gave her a revelation. A sense of life as more profound, less dependable, perhaps more transcendent broke through. Now she realizes that her former notion of reality was inadequate and wonders how to remain aware of the deeper, less predictable one. She does not call it God, but wishes to integrate her new experience of the absurd and irrational into her life, not because it is useful, merely because it is true. She grapples with becoming poor in spirit.

I know another woman who had just gotten out of prison with a bus ticket and fifteen dollars to start her life again. The social service agency that had placed her three children in foster care while she was in prison rented an apartment for her and brought her children back to her the day after she returned. Two days after that she called me because she needed to move again: the apartment heater had a dangerous open gas flame, and the landlord refused to fix it. Without money, my friend had miraculously found another apartment, but had no way to move her few pieces of furniture. As we stood on the street by the phone booth in the rain, trying to call someone with a pickup truck, I remarked that she seemed quite calm. She merely looked at me and said, "It's necessity."

Her use of the word "necessity" reminded me of Simone Weil, for whom necessity is what the slave feels in the presence of the master, what the utterly poor and dependent soul feels in the presence of God. Each must wait patiently for the slightest indication of what the master wishes or intends to have done.

One observes in every sort of circumstance that patience practiced by my friend standing in the rain. It is the patience parents have with prodigal children, drug abusers or runaways. They cannot lift a hand to change their children's behavior or bring them home, and yet they continue to love and hope for them. It is the patience of war refugees interned in camps far from their homes, or of victims of natural disasters who return to the places their homes used to be, calmly sorting through the rubble to find what is usable.

The old rule of the Congregation of the Oratory exhorted its members to pray from this patient posture: "When we are at prayer we should think and act as do the poor. When they knock at a door they wait patiently until something is brought to them; then, avoiding anything like importunity, they knock again."

The opposite of this total dependence on God, poverty of spirit, is the search for security in people, places, and things that are not God. In our culture we rely primarily on ourselves. We moderns don't need God. We construct our own salvation and, like the Pharisees, we build it on the law: human law, the law of the land, courts of law, scientific laws, the rules of technology, psychology, politics, and sports. We live by the rules, trusting that others will also, and punishing them when they don't. How else can life be made fair? We have it in our capable human hands to do justice through the law, to keep things even, to ward off chaos.

In Robert Bolt's play based on the life of Saint Thomas More, *A Man for All Seasons*, Bolt has More reply to the zealot William Roper who claims that he'd cut down every law in England to get to the devil:

> Oh? And when the last law was down, and the Devil turned on you—where would you hide, Roper, the laws all being flat? This country's planted thick with laws from coast to coast—Man's laws, not God's—and if you cut them down ... d'you really think you could stand upright in the

winds that would blow then? Yes, I'd give the Devil
benefit of law, for my own safety's sake.

More's view is eloquent, sensible, wise. And yet eventually the laws—including one that would have saved his
life—are flattened by Henry VIII. More finally gives his life
not for the law, but for God's truth.

The song sung by the policeman Javert in the musical
version of *Les Miserables* is an enchanting statement of the
virtues of dependence on the law. In a lovely melody, Javert
calls on the stars as symbol of order and light. He compares
those who break the law to falling stars. Like Lucifer, they
burst into flame and fall.

And so it's written on the doorways to Paradise
that those who falter and those who fall
must pay the price.

Powerful as it is, this song's message withers in the bright
light of the life of the hero Jean Valjean, who risks his freedom
to protect a child given to his care by her prostitute mother.
In Victor Hugo's story, as in life, the law is inadequate. It is
pharisaical. To live by a set of principles rather than by love
is to render ourselves unprepared for the vagaries and shocks
of existence, which does not play by the rules. Javert himself,
utterly committed to the rule of law, kills himself at the
humiliation of receiving mercy from the criminal Valjean.
Mercy, like love, violates the rules.

From modern science we know that principles, even the
laws of the physical universe, are not so immutable as once
was believed. We can think of them as statements that merely
approximate reality. Straight lines are really curves, matter is
really energy, and time bends like the magic wand of a
carnival roustabout. We had better learn to bend (or squat
like the poor) with it, to rely not on law but on mystery, if we
are not to break or be broken.

Failing to depend on God, we succumb to dependence
on other human creations less noble than the law. We fall in
love with the works of our hands, like the first human who

crafted something for the joy of possessing rather than using or admiring it. We Americans make gods of our goods on a grander scale than most because of the sheer availability of consumer goods and the worship of them institutionalized by advertising. "Datsun Saves," cars are "Infiniti," and we pray, "Help me, Honda." Our children will not go to school without designer labels in their clothing, and millions of people's working lives—decades of their time on earth that might otherwise be spent building up society—are eaten up in the production of junk.

Our goods dwarf us. Their production rapidly converts the earth's resources into trash. The time and energy spent acquiring and using them enervates us. In his play *The Price*, Arthur Miller has one character say:

> What is the key word today? Disposable. The more you can throw it away the more it's beautiful. This car, the furniture, the wife, the children—everything has to be disposable. Because you see the main thing today is—shopping. Years ago a person, he was unhappy, didn't know what to do with himself—he'd go to church, start a revolution—*something*. Today you're unhappy? Can't figure it out? What is the salvation? Go shopping.

Shopping is America's salvation. I live in a part of the country about to be smothered by malls. They look more and more like the contemporary equivalent of medieval cathedrals, complete with holiday shrines and lights directing the eye to icons for veneration. People visit malls when they have nowhere else to go, because they have to get out of the house, walk, be around other people yet not engaged with them. They may also want to cheer themselves up with a purchase. The malls are open when churches are closed. They are especially full around holidays like Christmas and Easter, which originated in the church's cycle of celebration but now anchor the annual spending cycle that makes the economy hum. Our economy is "saved" by Christmas and

Easter, even as we are not. We have come to depend on our goods, not on our God.

This consumerism is violent as well as banal. Locally, it spawns teen-agers who shoot one another for the gold chains or fashionable sneakers they wear. Globally, it prompts population programs for poor countries that have "too many people" for the earth to sustain, ignoring the fact that one consumer in the developed world uses more resources than ten in the so-called developing world. As the author of the epistle of James says, greed is the root of these conflicts:

> What causes conflicts and quarrels among you? Do they not spring from the aggressiveness of your bodily desires? You want something which you cannot have, and so you are bent on murder; you are envious and cannot attain your ambition, and so you quarrel and fight" (Jas 4:1-2).

The ultimate thing we depend on instead of God is our weapons. They promise us security even in the absence of housing, health care, and social welfare. In the book of Judges Yahweh three times pares down Gideon's army of Israelites, reducing it from 32,000 to 300 men to make abundantly clear that the Israelites cannot win a war against the Midianites without Yahweh's help. Their trust must be in Yahweh, not in their own might. In the "real world" however, we can't trust God to defend us from our enemies. Thus the irony that the most churchgoing nation in the world maintains the largest arsenal in the world.

During the 1980s American Catholic bishops wrote pastoral letters exhorting peace and asking critical questions about military policy and expenditures, yet they could never bring themselves to condemn the doctrine of nuclear deterrence, founded on the threat and the ability to kill millions of people. They could not relinquish that "security." When they did speak out against a specific war—the war against Iraq, for example—they continued to speak in generalities even as the bombs fell. Yet bishops seem surprised when they are not heeded. They wonder why their flocks do not follow. Could it be that they do not lead clearly, early, and decisively enough? The gods of military security that have captured the trust of millions will not be toppled by mere words and belated gestures.

The kingdom of heaven that blesses the poor in spirit is not the "real world" of negotiation, deterrence, just war theories, or "collateral damage." And yet it is the real world. The real Jesus says, "Blessed are the poor in spirit, theirs is the kingdom of heaven." The Greek *basileus* from the Hebrew *melek* means "kingdom" or "reign," and "heaven" is a roundabout way of saying "God." The kingdom of heaven is not a place, nor is it a utopia; it is a relationship between God and human beings, between God and the poor in particular.

The reign of God occurs not in the future but in the bliss of the poor at the very moment they suffer and yet remain faithful, learning through their suffering to depend more and more for their joy only on God. Theirs is the bliss of the Psalmist who sings,

Let me dwell in thy tent forever!

Oh to be safe under the shelter of thy wings (Ps 61:4).

It is the trust of Job who, after losing everything, concludes, "I knew of thee then only by report, but now I see thee with my own eyes" (Jb 42:5).

Simone Weil also speaks of the present blessedness of the poor:

> We cannot under any circumstances manufacture something which is better than ourselves. This effort truly stretched toward goodness cannot reach its goal; it is after long, fruitless effort which ends in despair, when we no longer expect anything, that, from outside ourselves, the gift comes as a marvelous surprise. The effort has destroyed a part of the false sense of fullness within us. The divine emptiness, fuller than fullness, has come to inhabit us (Weil, *Gravity and Grace*, p. 94).

As he waited for his prodigal son, the father knew divine emptiness. He went beyond despair. He became expectant, hopeful in the deepest sense. Had he not been, he could not have welcomed the return with spontaneous celebration. Parents like him know that God lives in their children, no matter how far astray, and they never cease to wait patiently. Theirs is not unlike the stubborn peace known by other parents who, despite limited resources, take in extra children simply because they see the children's needs. They risk straining the family budget and even some family relationships by harboring those for whom there may be rationally no room. Nevertheless, they reap the bliss of the one who depends on God alone.

The bliss of the poor gifted Jesus and the Buddha, Teresa of Avila and John of the Cross. It is the joy of the alcoholic and prisoner who acknowledge their helplessness and decide to change, of the peasant woman in Honduras who thanks God for the grain to make tortillas for one more day, of the refugee in Jordan who praises Allah for reuniting his family despite the fact that they still must live in a refugee camp. Only to the onlooker does the sweetness of the moment seem out of all proportion to the wretched circumstances of their lives.

Artist Fritz Eichenberg, whose wood engravings graced *The Catholic Worker* for thirty years, speaks of the experience of living in the reign of God:

> The artist who wants to serve God will have to embrace poverty. There must be quite a few who embrace poverty, unsung in our pagan world. Yet, I think those are the happy ones, happy as only those can be who live an integrated life, worshiping as they work, creating when they feel inspired, freely giving of their talent without counting the pennies of their reward (Eichenberg, p. 4).

"Share! So that you may be happy," said Salvadoran martyr Archbishop Oscar Romero in a 1980 homily for the

Feast of the Epiphany. Speaking to the rich people of El Salvador, he pleaded with them not to idolize their wealth and let the poor die of hunger. "We must know how to strip ourselves of our rings so they won't cut off our fingers. ... Whoever isn't willing to do without his rings risks having them cut off his hand. Whoever is unwilling to give out of love and social justice makes mandatory that his luxuries be taken away by violence." Romero, like the evangelist Luke, proclaims a woe to the rich. As the obverse of his beatitude, Luke tells them they have already had their happiness (6:24). They do not invite the poor and lame to their feasts (14:12-14); they exalt themselves and do not live in right relationship with others and consequently do not know the reign of God.

On the other hand, the poor who might have cause to curse the darkness, instead give thanks and praise, and are blessed with the kingdom of heaven. Denizens of the "real world" call them naive, dreamers, ineffectual, but they are nonetheless more blessed, more blissful than those who scramble for security in the normal places. Because it is true, this deeper reality that we have finally, after all our resistance, come to rely upon when we are poor blesses us with what someone has called the "bliss of the destitute."

In his poem, "When in the Soul of the Serene Disciple," Thomas Merton writes of this bliss:

> When in the soul of the serene disciple
> With no more Fathers to imitate
> Poverty is a success,
> It is a small thing to say the roof is gone:
> He has not even a house.
>
> Stars, as well as friends,
> Are angry with the noble ruin.
> Saints depart in several directions.
>
> Be still:
> There is no longer any need of comment.

It was a lucky wind
That blew away his halo with his cares,
A lucky sea that drowned his reputation.

Here you will find
Neither a proverb nor a memorandum.
There are no ways,
No methods to admire
Where poverty is no achievement.
His God lives in his emptiness like an affliction.

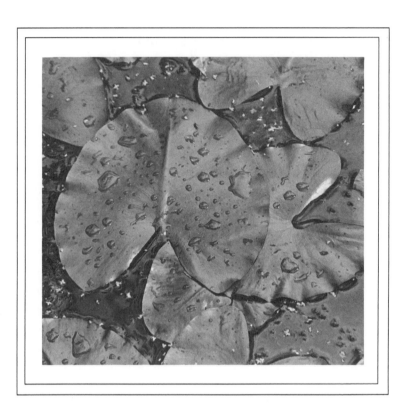

2

Blessed Are They Who Mourn

In some traditions, notably in the Middle East, the mourner must demonstrate sorrow at a time of death in order to assure the peace of the loved one who has died. Loud lamentations, the rending of garments, beating one's breast, these and other actions are the expected behavior at funerals and recall the grieving for Joseph by his father Jacob who "rent his clothes, put on sackcloth and mourned his son for a long time" (Gn 37:34). In western culture we tend to view such behavior as undignified and to admire instead the mourner who quietly goes about the funeral preparations, keeps a "stiff upper lip," and generally gives the sense of one whose feelings lie too deep for human tears.

Such cultural expectations in the West may or may not have their roots in Christian theology, but it is true that the resurrection of Jesus, foreshadowing the resurrection of all believers and doers of the word, would seem to militate against the most desperate feelings of loss and despair at the death of a loved one. If my dearest love has died, and I believe in a resurrection into life after death, how can I mourn as deeply as someone who believes the loss is absolutely final? If I rend my garments and beat my breast, am I not making a lie of my proclaimed belief in the resurrection?

No matter how profound my Christian belief, however, the death and departure of those I love cause me to ache as much as any atheist or animist. Whatever I believe will happen again in the future cannot compensate for the immediate and heart-rending loss, not only of the person I love, but also of the way of life we had together. The world cannot go on for me in the same way when I lose a part of my life, and the loss reminds me of my own and all mortality, the fragility of all arrangements, the potential shipwreck of all expectations. Thus the Greek word *pentheo* used for mourning in the beatitudes is the strongest word for mourning in the language and denotes this passionate lament for the dead.

Most adults, and many children, have experienced the sense of total loss. At some point in our lives we are all mourners. For those who have enough power, charm, good looks, and talent to avert much pain and suffering, death or separation from a loved one may be the one deep sorrow that is unavoidable. Then we all feel the ache, the cavity at the center of our being, the elusive lump carried somewhere between the chest and the throat that slows both our movements and our thoughts, suspending them in midair, making us unfit for company. We feel with the psalmist who cries, "From the end of the earth I call to thee with fainting heart" (Ps 61:2).

Jesus, who rose himself and brought others back from the dead, mourned. Even as he assured Martha that no one with faith would ever die, he sighed deeply and wept to know that her brother and his friend Lazarus lay in the tomb. He wept also for Jerusalem, mourning the fate of "the city that murders the prophets and stones the messengers sent to her" (Mt 23:37). He offers the image of himself as a mother hen longing to gather her brood under her wings, trying in vain to protect her innocents from the evildoers. The brooding mother hen, longing but unable to gather all her chicks, typifies the frustration and emptiness of those confronted with the absurdity of loss.

Absurdity is key here. The mourner comes face to face with the fact that life is not logical, that reality is deaf to the voice of reason, and that even though we feel in our deepest being that the universe is finally friendly, its up-front manifestations often fly in the face of kindness and common sense. Why does a child suffer? Why do the cruel prosper? Why do hurricanes, tornadoes, and other natural disasters seem mainly to afflict the poor? We may glance at these questions in our everyday lives, but we are normally too busy getting breakfast for the family, making deadlines at work, worrying about tax preparation in April to allow ourselves much rumination on the eternal verities. Death, separation, divorce, a child's severe illness; such events barge into our lives and change all that, forcing us to think in universal terms of why and how things work or don't seem to work.

These thoughts can lead, despite all the evidence, to breakthroughs in human experience and development. The Buddha's royal father organized life in his kingdom so his son would never see suffering. But as a result of his son's first encounter with old age in the form of a tottering beggar on the road, he became the world's greatest teacher whose teaching was based precisely on the human response to suffering. Similarly, the great work of artists and philosophers often flows from their reactions to and insight about the nature of suffering. Michelangelo's *Pieta* and Picasso's *Guernica* immediately come to mind.

Because it is a truth that sometimes has to break through our comfortable but false notions of reality, suffering can be a gift. Spanish philosopher Jose Ortega y Gasset describes the lengths we will go to to avoid facing reality:

> Even a person's "ideas" are merely the individual's blinders before reality, a way of avoiding the sight of his own life. ... The individual suspects as much, but is terrified to encounter this frightening reality face to face, and so attempts to conceal it by drawing a curtain of fantasy over it. ... The fact that his

"ideas" are not true does not worry him: he employs them as redoubts from behind which he can defend himself from life; or he uses them as a form of bravado to scare off reality (Ortega y Gasset, pp. 142-143).

What is it that the bravado is guarding? What can the crashing of death and separation into our lives deliver us from? What possible good can mourning lead to? The bravado protects our egos. And mourning can deliver us from ego-centeredness, that selfishness we are all heir to and need to spend our lives shaking ourselves loose from. When Jesus wept for the fate of Jerusalem, his tears bespoke a concern for others that rendered him vulnerable. When he wept for Lazarus, he was truly alive, moved by the plight of one outside himself. He was a normal, feeling person, in other words, and his example should make us hesitate when we are tempted to say to children, more often little boys, that they shouldn't cry.

Mourning can also help us become the contemplative persons we are meant to be. It stops us in our tracks, urging us to interrupt our fast-paced and thoughtless lives to take the hesitant and reflective stance some situations call for. "Don't just do something, stand there," says the teacher, speaking to the most intractable situations. Given the pragmatism of our culture, however, if we are not actively avoiding a problem, we are busy bustling about it till we can say we have solved that one, all right, and quickly too.

It takes courage to admit the insolubility of a problem and to strike out into the dark of contemplation, from which an eventual solution or an alternative situation may or may not develop. It means to employ Mary, not Martha, when the kitchen is full of bubbling pots. But if we are busy fussing about the pots, we put in doubt the possibility of long-range solutions to the perpetual kitchen mess.

In recent years we have seen on our television screens pictures of birds and other animals coated with oil from spills in Alaska, the Persian Gulf, the Mediterranean, and the North

Sea, oil that kills the animals by cutting them off from oxygen. In many cases nothing can be done for them except to mourn them. Perhaps from the mourning we may eventually develop the capacity for feeling rooted in attention, a contemplative stance on their behalf and on our own. We may yet learn the interdependence we have with animals and perhaps develop ways of human living that don't endanger the earth.

It is painful to know we cannot wash the oil from millions of dying animals, painful also to watch thousands of Kurds die on an unreachable mountainside as they flee a country in turmoil stirred up by a war instigated by our own nation. Painful to hear in our dreams the cries of Bosnian women being raped. But sometimes we must watch in order to learn what we must know and do.

Late one summer night some years ago, I drove through New York's Harlem with a friend who advised me to keep my eyes closed as we passed through one section. Something within me that was more than idle curiosity—I do not go to scary movies, watch rescue shows on TV, or stare at highway collisions—resisted closing my eyes. Other people had to live with the reality outside those car windows; who was I to feel I had a right to avoid merely observing it as I passed by? It occurred to me then that the definition of a contemplative might be one who keeps eyes open to reality, no matter how horrible the sight or helpless the feeling it engenders.

Certainly Vedran Smailovic, mentioned in a recent *Catholic Worker* news item, is a contemplative. In May 1992 at about four o'clock in the afternoon, twenty-two people were killed by Serbian mortar fire while standing in line outside a bakery in Sarajevo. For the next twenty-two days, Smailovic, a cellist in the Sarajevo Symphony, brought his chair and cello to that deserted street at four o'clock and, "with Serbian shells crashing around him, played Albinoni's 'Adagio' to honor each person who had died." In the midst of barbarity, Smailovic's mourning refuses to allow us to think that all humanity has died.

Some people and some situations are so difficult, important, or wonderful that "attention must be paid," as Arthur Miller has Mrs. Willie Loman say in *Death of a Salesman*. Attention must be paid to a reality beyond ourselves that pulls us there. Attention must be paid because it is from careful attention to a person or situation that we enter into a relationship that enables us to understand, whether we understand in order to change or to celebrate. And mourning may be the way reality gets our attention.

The opposite of mourning is numbness, repression, denial, forgetting, amnesia. We know what it is *not* to be able to cry, to be so overwhelmed by an onslaught of grief or horror that we have no immediate response to it. If that numbness persists, we risk becoming automatons. Many experience a loved one's funeral as a time of going through the motions. They may objectify themselves to the point where they seem to observe themselves acting a role. Only after the public performance, alone or with family and friends, are they able to cry or speak their feelings.

Sometimes grief requires that we ask pardon of the dead. We promise them they won't be forgotten, or resolve to change our own lives in a way the loved one would have wished. Implicit in the beatitude is repentance, sorrow for one's own sin or unworthiness. If we mourn a loss like divorce or rupture from parents or children, we may need to ponder a sequence of events, the behavior of many years perhaps, that led up to it. Above all, we must not close down our minds and hearts in order to move ahead quickly after death or separation. It may be years before we can grasp its full meaning, and meanwhile life must go on. But unless we allow time specifically for mourning, for both feeling and pondering, we do not move ahead in a fruitful manner.

Mourning also moves us to forgive. I live in a state that inflicts the death penalty, and whenever we have an execution, often six or eight years after the original murder, family members of the murder victim come before the cameras to affirm that the execution is a good thing and long overdue.

The murder of their loved one demands this retribution. Other citizens, some for and some against the execution, demonstrate in front of the prison. The noisier ones shout that murderers on death row should be killed more quickly. They intend to hallow the memory of the victim, but their barbaric rituals attendant on the even more barbaric one of capital punishment assure that the victim will be remembered mainly for having been murdered. Instead of moving into history as a human being with family, friends, talents, and purpose, he or she arrives there labelled as a victim.

I know a man whose wife was brutally murdered by someone who thus rendered himself eligible for the death penalty. My friend, who had spent his life teaching poor youth, petitioned that the murderer not be charged with a capital crime. He could not bear that his gentle wife be remembered for another person's death in her name. He did not want her, with all her goodness and accomplishment, recalled in news articles primarily as the victim of the criminal on death row. For the sake of his wife, whom he mourned deeply, he had to forgive.

Organizations, even nations, need to mourn. Some projects and groups outlive their original purposes and should die and be mourned in a manner that allows acknowledgment of their contributions. Instead of facilitating mourning, however, some organizational leaders continue to call meetings, promote new projects, and even discourage re-examination of the group's goals. A friend of mine belonged for years to a faculty wives' club that hosted monthly luncheons to encourage socializing among departmental wives. In a new era of two-career households, long after most of the faculty wives were working at their own jobs (some teaching at the same university as their husbands), club leaders continued to expect all departmental wives to be available for lunches once a month. They failed to see the new reality that called for a decent burial and perhaps some mourning for the club.

Other women's groups that once relied on the time and volunteer labor of women not working outside the home have closed out their organizations with due mourning and even some panache. Still others, like the League of Women Voters, recognizing that the need for the organization remains, have adopted more flexible scheduling and new membership policies that encourage working women and men, especially retired men with time, to join. Earlier members may regret the passing of the old forms, but out of mourning has come new life.

Many Roman Catholic religious communities, mourning the loss of vocations to the traditional lifetime commitment to the vows, have expanded their membership to include families and singles who make temporary commitments to the group. They have also merged efforts with those of similar groups. Some argue against this, saying it will change the nature of religious community, but others say that this change may be resurrectional and precisely what the future demands. Sorting through priorities in the process of making the changes has actually clarified for many groups their original purposes.

Meanwhile, other communities clearly in their death throes have made no conscious attempt either to die gracefully or to meet the future. Individuals within them may engage in mourning, but the group's denial of the need for corporate mourning leaves it paralyzed and its members living two-dimensional lives together.

Nations also need to mourn. President Abraham Lincoln's great gift was his leadership in mourning during the Civil War. When asked to give a speech at the Gettysburg battlefield where thousands had died bloody deaths and were left ill-buried, he spoke 272 words that reframed the Constitution in the principle of equality enunciated in the Declaration of Independence. In his *Lincoln at Gettysburg: The Words That Remade America*, Garry Wills shows how the address epitomized Lincoln's views of war and death and the Union. The president of all the people mentioned no foes, exhibited no anger, gave no rebuke. He rose "above the particular, the local, and the divisive" and used a biblical vocabulary to express the suffering and resurrection of a chosen people.

In Wills' view the Gettysburg Address must be supplemented with the Second Inaugural Address where Lincoln brings sin into the picture:

The Almighty has his own purposes.
"Woe unto the world because of offenses!
For it must needs be that offenses come;
but woe to that man by whom the offense cometh."

Lincoln saw a mysterious Providence at work in the war and proclaimed a series of fast days and thanksgiving day times of repentance for the whole nation's sins of violence. Unlike most leaders who ratchet up the claims as the war goes on, says Wills, Lincoln ratcheted them down.

In the Second Inaugural, he asked:

With malice toward none;
with charity for all:
with firmness in the right,
as God gives us to see the right,
let us strive on
to finish the work we are in;
to bind up the nation's wounds;
to care for him who shall have borne the battle,
    and for his widow, and his orphan—
to do all which may achieve
    and cherish
    a just, and a lasting peace,
among ourselves, and with all nations.

Lincoln's mourning is both comforting and a work of peacemaking.

Despite his reluctance to outlaw slavery because such an action might threaten the Union, Lincoln thought it a great evil. Proponents of slavery who wanted to spread it to more territories had caused the Mexican War as well as the Civil War, he believed. A melancholic person, he struggled with the war's meaning and communicated his mourning and sense of meaning to the American people. Wills concludes that Lincoln revolutionized the American Revolution, appealing to the spirit rather than the letter of the Constitution, which tolerated slavery. He was thereby able to give people "a new past to live with that would change their future indefinitely."

Since Lincoln, we have had little leadership for public mourning in America. As a nation we have not repented our war crimes at Hiroshima and Nagasaki. President Truman called the dropping of the atom bomb a great day for our country, and no subsequent president has countered his words. Recent financial reimbursements to Japanese Americans interned in U.S. concentration camps during World War II do express some symbolic remorse for sins against them. They may represent, however obliquely, an attempt to mourn.

It appears that Germany has better mourned its role in World War II than the United States has mourned either Hiroshima or the Vietnam War. American writers, artists, and filmmakers have tried to awaken the nation to mourn for Vietnam. Neil Sheehan's *A Bright and Shining Lie: John Paul Vann and Vietnam* is a mammoth and eloquent dirge for the deaths from political hubris. Films like *Apocalypse Now, The Deer Hunter,* and *The Killing Fields* evoke a kind of secular repentance for the evil done by our Vietnam adventure. Religious and secular groups working against U.S. intervention in Central America often wish to "prevent another Vietnam." Prevention can be a form of repentance.

But our public policy continues to reflect the desire to forget rather than mourn the Vietnam War. We see this in the long and bitter struggles for compensation for veterans suffering with the aftermath of Agent Orange, Posttraumatic Stress Syndrome, or drug addiction incurred as a result of duty in Vietnam. Far from calling for mourning, our political

leaders have generally reflected our national desire for amnesia; except when they obliquely admit to a loss, as when
President George Bush bombed Iraq to compensate for Vietnam!

Germany, on the other hand, has acknowledged its loss
and publicly repented its role in the Holocaust. Most German
artists and historians have emphasized German guilt. The
student revolts of the sixties are widely thought to have been
a reaction to the parents' history of Nazism. A 1955 poll in
Der Spiegel at the height of the Cold War, showed that more
than three-quarters of the German people preferred not to
see soldiers in German uniform.

Especially in public speech and public policy the contrast
between Germany after World War II and the U.S. after
Vietnam is stark. In October 1945, in what came to be known
as the Stuttgart Pronouncement, the Evangelical Church for-
mally acknowledged "not only a great community of suffering with our people but also a solidarity of guilt. With great
pain we say: Because of us, infinite suffering has been visited
on many peoples and countries." The church did fight the
spirit of National Socialism, they continued, "but we hold
ourselves culpable for not confessing more courageously, for
not praying more faithfully, for not believing more joyously,
for not loving more ardently" (Stern, p. 190n).

Conscious of its militaristic past, until recently Germany
committed troops only to NATO and restricted arms sales
abroad.

As East-West tensions lessened, even German soldiers—
now trained to discuss orders before following them—felt it
was time to cut back the military presence in Europe. Since
World War II West Germany had resettled millions of
refugees and, according to Amity Shlaes in *Germany: The
Empire Within*, in the seventies and eighties took in thousands
of candidates for political asylum from places as far away as
Ethiopia and Sri Lanka, in the conviction that Germany, with
its record of political persecution under the Nazis, now ought
to serve as a model of political tolerance (Shlaes, p. 19).

In recent years, with the economic burdens entailed in the reuniting of the Germanies at a time of worldwide recession, the presence of large numbers of refugees has become more troublesome and some German voices remind the world of other-than-German sins against humanity, but much public policy still reflects the repentance that accompanies mourning.

The United States, on the other hand, expresses at best ambiguity toward its Vietnam adventure. Erecting a moving memorial to Americans killed in Vietnam, it has not publicly remembered nor regretted the Vietnamese killed in the war. On the contrary, our government holds the Vietnamese government to a much higher standard than its enemies in earlier wars as we seek an accounting for every single military person missing in action in Vietnam. When we cease relentless pursuit of the MIAs and add the names of Vietnamese to the Vietnam Memorial, we may as a nation begin to mourn, acknowledging that we and the Vietnamese are tragically bound together as were the northerners and southerners Lincoln addressed.

Confusion and lack of leadership, among other things, have kept us from mourning our involvement in Vietnam, but this failure diminishes us as a nation just as it would diminish an individual. One consequence of mourning the Vietnam War might be wisdom to avoid similar adventures in the future. Santayana said that those who do not learn from history are condemned to repeat it. One could paraphrase his famous aphorism, "Those who do not mourn their history will be condemned to repeat it." Mourning brings to memory the dimension of the heart, and in the case of a society that has inflicted pain, the willingness to ask forgiveness and to change.

As troublesome in its own way as the Vietnam Memorial is Yad Vaashem, the historically accurate and aesthetically arresting Holocaust memorial in Jerusalem. Its title from Isaiah 56 means "memory and a name," and it gives that to millions of Holocaust victims. To visit Yad Vaashem, especially the Children's Memorial, is to revisit the worst that we as humans are capable of. Yad Vaashem is a great and detailed act of human memory. Room after room of photographs, films, clothing, jewelry, letters, audio tapes, and other memorabilia of Holocaust victims grip the visitor's attention. The words of the great rabbi Baal Shem Tov, "Forgetfulness leads to Exile, while remembrance is the secret of redemption," are invoked there. But Yad Vaashem nevertheless omits what mourning must include in the name of the victims, some gesture of forgiveness. Without that, there is no redemption. Consequently, although it memorializes, Yad Vaashem fails to mourn.

Like our Vietnam Memorial in Washington, a moving but partial statement by a frustrated offender not yet capable of repentance, Yad Vaashem is a haunting but partial statement by a victim not yet capable of forgiveness. It may be that Israel, unable to feel secure, like an abused spouse or child unable to get distance from the abuser, until recently has been incapable of forgiving. Nevertheless, it must forgive, truly mourn, in order to be healed. The Vietnam Memorial and Yad Vaashem both give significant but flawed testimonies. One belongs to a people that continues to prosecute wars against smaller nations; the other, to a people that has treated Palestinians as the Nazis treated Jews. Like individuals unable to mourn, both America and Israel risk remaining stuck in a two-dimensional and uncomforted existence.

Having said that mourning can gift us with contemplation, I would add that it should lead beyond contemplation to action. What we see when we look at the pain of the world leads us to act on behalf of those who suffer. A seminary professor I met, wishing his students to incorporate concern for poor people into their future ministries, offered a course in which students read dozens of books about hunger. They also wrote papers, delivered sermons, and had prayer services about hunger.

At the end of the semester the professor felt assured that some of the students had an exhaustive knowledge of hunger in this country and abroad. They had studied its causes and effects, as well as large and small scale efforts to alleviate it. They were concerned about hungry people. The hitch was, they felt paralyzed. Because they had acquired so much information and had also become aware of the dangers of counterproductive action, they felt that hunger was too big and intractable a problem to solve.

The professor, dismayed by the students' paralysis, finally concluded that his error lay in not requiring the students to take some action against hunger. Inaction, he realized, is as senseless and debilitating as mere knee-jerk responses. Not one student had written to a Congressperson to urge improvement of U.S. food programs, not one had helped out in a soup kitchen, not one had organized a canned goods collection in church. As a result of their failure to act, these future ministers remain as ill-prepared to lead their congregations on behalf of the poor as those who have never given hunger a thought and will merely allow the congregation to pay its annual dues to the poor by making up food baskets at Thanksgiving.

If the students had acted on the suffering caused by hunger, had fasted or lobbied or helped to feed someone, they would have been better equipped to walk a middle path between those who spin their wheels on superficial projects that fail to address hunger's causes and those who ignore the problem. Their cerebral study was not mourning and could not bring comfort to themselves or others.

People in El Salvador have mourned much and have much to mourn. They soon learn the meaning of the beatitude. In 1989, after more than 70,000 had died in the previous decade, mostly from government violence, I was struck by how many people repeated the sentence, "We feel the violence in our own flesh." Their reflections made in the light of the gospel, also prompted another frequently spoken phrase, "The martyrs make the space for us to act." Whether the director of the Human Rights Office for the Archdiocese of San Salvador or the mother of a young man mutilated and left to die on the road, each who spoke these words affirmed that even seemingly senseless suffering and death, taken into the heart, may clear an unexpected path.

Theirs was not the warrior's claim that because so many have died in a war, ceasing to fight would render the sacrifice of the dead useless. Salvadorans truly wanted peace and knew it by its absence. Theirs was the comprehension that death ruptures the life of the whole community and that sacrificial death gives back some new creative energy, some "space" for taking the next step. Their life in community allowed many Salvadorans comfort, even in the midst of mourning.

Community is central to the promise of the beatitude, "Blessed are they who mourn, for they shall be comforted." When I have sorrowed for a long time, mourning diminishment or death, the first light penetrating the darkness of my pain comes from the lamp carried by another. A friend reaches out once again, and I am at last able to see the extended, faithful hand. Or I observe at a distance some other human gesture, a flower given, a father's interaction with his child, or a startling human bridging of the many fissures cutting through our lives together.

Suddenly some of the clouds disperse, and I can move again. Later I say that God brought me peace, consoled me. Consolation, comfort is the peace of God returned to our lives even as we mourn. It is the resurrection in the midst of death, rejoicing even in the midst of loss.

Ironically, people who do not take time to mourn are often those who cannot take time to rejoice. The poor throw the best parties. The parent most weighed down by her own father's recent death may be the one careful to see that her child's birthday does not get overlooked in the surrounding sorrow. In El Salvador, refugees from a hurricane living in cardboard and tin shacks gave one of the liveliest fiestas I have attended. Those who carefully trace the many faces of death know most surely that life and its celebrations must go on.

Jean Vanier, founder of international communities including the mentally and physically handicapped, thinks
that encountering the poor will change us more than
knowledge about them, and that community is grounded
more firmly in weakness than strength. "Unfortunately, we
have developed such a power of independent-ism," he says.
"We have been taught that we must defend and protect
ourselves so as not to be abandoned. Whereas, community is
a completely different thing. It is a lowering of those barriers,
becoming vulnerable, and therefore ready to be hurt if the
other leaves" (Vanier, p. 21). Ready to be hurt. Ready to
mourn.

If we can mourn, if we are vulnerable, if we can con-
template and forgive and act, we can be community and be
comforted. Individuals can get on with their lives, somewhat
healed, somewhat more able to heal others. Organizations
and nations can get beyond the fixations that bind them to
the same old wheel of error. If we can mourn, death and
diminishment become more graced and graceful; and we
gather new life together, life more profound for having
embraced the unavoidable pain. Our comfort then is resurrection. Today.

3

Blessed Are the Meek

The great Irish-American labor organizer Mother Jones, known for her feisty stances and pithy sayings, received few accolades for meekness. Once, exiting a jailhouse where she had visited an imprisoned miner, she commented, "He's in for stealing a pair of shoes. If he'd stolen a railroad, they'd make him a U.S. Senator." On another occasion, perhaps unwittingly describing her own vocation, she advised, "Pray for the dead and fight like hell for the living." Were meekness understood rightly, we might see Mother Jones as exemplifying it.

The Greek word *praus* used in the earliest translations of the beatitudes is one of the great Greek ethical words for the golden mean sought by the philosophers, in this case the mean between excessive anger and complete lack of anger. In today's psychological terminology, we might think of the extremes as arrogance and passive aggression and the mean as a healthy assertiveness. In the beatitude Jesus was proclaiming in a sense, "Blessed is the one who knows when it is appropriate to feel and to express anger."

Jesus echoes Psalm 37, an admonition to cease anger and envy and to hope in the Lord because "the humble shall possess the land," but Jesus himself was not without anger. He was not servile, as many think the meek and gentle are. He taught his followers to turn the other cheek, but he also drove the money changers out of the temple and spoke

assertively to authorities on a number of occasions, notably
when one of the High Priest's police struck him while he was
being interrogated. His response, "If I spoke amiss, state it in
evidence; if I spoke well, why strike me?" (Jn 18:23), was no
less feisty than some of Mother Jones'.

In his commentary on the gospel of Matthew, William
Barclay points out that *praus* was also the word used to
describe a domesticated animal or a person with great self-
control. Such self-control is exemplified by the Stoics, so
admired by the Romans and eloquently summed up in the
life and work of Marcus Aurelius, one of the few Roman
emperors history links with peaceful pursuits. No doubt
such self-control is admirable and rare. How many of us can
say as Marcus Aurelius does in his *Meditations* that we keep
our spirits "free from violence and unharmed, superior to
pains and pleasures, doing nothing without a purpose, nor
yet falsely and with hypocrisy, not feeling the need of another
man's doing or not doing anything"? Marcus Aurelius'
Stoicism represents in the West the epitome of the virtue of
self-control.

But for Jesus, meekness is more God-control than self-
control: the gentle one refrains from aggression but not from
asserting the case for God and God's special concerns in the
world. We know from Isaiah that meekness does not break
the bruised reed, nor does it shout in the streets unless it
shouts the word of God on behalf of the poor and the broken-
hearted.

The meek person is humble, not arrogant or a know-it-all.
He or she knows the need to learn and the limits of the human
condition. The meek one is not Agamemnon but Moses. To
the Greeks Agamemnon was a great hero and king, but also
a tragic figure because he presumed divinity and refused to
heed the prophetess Cassandra. His daring to walk on a
purple robe, purple a color reserved for the gods, both sym-
bolized and occasioned his downfall in Aeschylus' tragic
drama named for him. Moses, on the other hand, a man not
unlike Agamemnon in his adventurism and resorting to

violence, was also "a man of great humility, the most humble man on earth" (Nm 12:3). God could do something with him.

We live in a time when many lament the absence of heroes and models for youth. A common plaint is that young people have only rock stars and basketball players to imitate. Not so. Extraordinary times always call forth extraordinary people, and the modern era has its share of genuine heroes. Some of them will never be known beyond their small circle of community, but many of them are identifiable as we look around our neighborhoods. The busy mother who sets up a baby-sitting co-op so that everyone's children can be cared for, the local minister who inspires his congregation to serve the poor, the trained nurse who organizes a hospice program or an AIDS ministry for her community or church—these are heroes and heroines for our time, especially when they calmly take on unpopular causes.

So also is Don Pedro, a Delegate of the Word I met in Honduras once. He is a campesino and supports himself and his large family, barely, by growing corn and beans. The local diocese trained him to read the Bible and lead discussions of it in rural villages where there is no priest. At prayer services he asks gentle but provocative questions to generate discussion among the villagers, many of whom cannot read. He walks dozens of miles on a Sunday to meet with a small group for a few hours. In their poverty the villagers live at the back end of the world, but Don Pedro, shoeless and nearly toothless, brings them his dignity and patience. He is meek.

Don Pedro: Delegado

You walk three miles
on mountain roads
to read the Word
imperfectly
with gaunt and Mayan
people of
no water

little food
less hope.

You stand before them
having nothing
but your self
and faith.
They stare at you intently
comprehending
that you stand for God.
The poor (and you)
have nothing else.

The mainline media, driven by commercial considerations, may not tell us about such heroes and heroines, but
books and the alternative press, often the religious press, will.
We do not have to settle or let our children settle for the
emulation of rock stars. We can bring into our homes and
conversations stories of local heroes as well as materials
about Mahatma Gandhi, Martin Luther King, Dorothy Day,
and others who model meekness for our children.

I mention these three public figures precisely because
they were not perfect. They were also not servile or passive.
But they were meek. Despite personal weakness or fragility,
they learned to respond appropriately to the structurally
violent situations endemic to our time. It helps to study third
century saints. It is more unsettling but ultimately more
fruitful to ponder the graces of contemporary ones. The
young Gandhi was a fop, for example. His lifelong harshness
toward women, especially his own wife, is fraught with
troublesome implications, but his "experiments with truth"
and guidance by *satyagraha* (or truth force) rather than his
own light allowed him to free his people from colonial rule.
He could sometimes drive his collaborators mad because he
seemed to them slow to take the obvious next step. In reality,
he was waiting on the truth. The meek one is not always sure
of knowing it.

Martin Luther King sometimes used women as sexual objects. At times he was also less than intellectually honest, employing the words of others without attribution in his graduate school papers. Nevertheless, he risked his life and reputation again and again, not so much to do what he thought was right but to do what God called him to do, and he consequently freed all Americans from the bondage of legalized segregation. His meekness was often tested most stringently by his friends and colleagues, as when ministers sympathetic to his cause criticized him for protesting at an "untimely" moment in Birmingham. In his "Letter from A Birmingham Jail" he writes to them that "shallow understanding from people of goodwill is more frustrating than absolute misunderstanding from people of ill will. Lukewarm acceptance is much more bewildering than outright rejection." This is meekness speaking, prompted by the truth and not by a pragmatic need to "keep the coalition together."

Similarly meek was Dorothy Day, a woman with some hard edges and intellectual inconsistencies (one Catholic Worker colleague said that they were all anarchists but Dorothy was the chief anarch). She would stand up against the state by doing civil disobedience on behalf of peace or farm-workers, but she would also allow herself to be taken to task by church authorities for real or imagined wrongs committed by her fellow community members. There was no more fervent critic of the inefficiency of community and its drain on the members' patience, yet she knew that without the inbuilt self-correction it brings, we may delude ourselves. Dorothy's consistency lay only in her fidelity to God and persistent community with the poor.

The opposite of meekness is the never-apologize, must-be-number-one syndrome that holds our nation in thrall. From their early years, American children, especially white males, learn competition and arrogance. Too many must be "number one" and struggle pathetically to look like Barbie doll or play basketball like Michael Jordan. Despite the efforts of some parents, schools, and churches to inculcate cooperation and gentleness, most children's exposure to the media, to school, and to athletics results in teen-agers at best confused, at worst barbaric, when it comes to respecting others and listening to the still small voice of truth. High rates of suicide, anorexia and bulimia, alcoholism, and drug use among the young testify to the extent of their confusion. Many parents today are satisfied when their children merely avoid addiction, depression, or serious clashes with the law.

Those who survive their youth have to negotiate an adult world where success is defined as knowing it all and having it all. If I have it all, I don't need the skills of negotiation and accommodation. If I know it all, I have nothing to learn and nothing to apologize for. Classified ads call for the "aggressive self-starter," energetic and at home in a "fast-paced environment." Some employers look for "team spirit," as do some athletic coaches. But all too often team spirit functions primarily to make the team number one. Judging by the want ads, there is no job market for those who think deeply, respect the contributions of others, and work patiently towards the achievement of long range goals. Embodying these latter gifts are many of the humble of the world, whom our culture might term unemployable.

I once saw a short documentary film that used scenes from a football game fading in and out of scenes from military training. The unstated but inescapable conclusion for the viewer was that the one was the preparation for the other. Not all the moves are the same, but all the attitudes are: rigorous discipline, victory through trickery or force, ranks closed against the opposition, the notion that "all's fair in ... ." Our games and too much our schools prepare young men and, increasingly, young women for military aggression and corporate competition. These settings leave little room for reflection on consequences.

As I write, the U.S. has just completed its hundred-hour air war against Iraq. The people of Iraq remain in turmoil, having been bombed back to a pre-industrial age. Some, who in the wake of the war rose up against their dictator, were left hanging on a freezing mountainside. Many still die each day, but for the U.S. the war is over, our troops coming home, our leaders claiming we have nothing to feel guilty about. Later we will learn that hundreds of thousands, mostly children, died because our bombs destroyed infrastructure, especially water and electrical systems. But euphoria holds at home. Parades are planned for many cities and towns. By our choice of military action over economic sanctions and diplomatic negotiations, we have invoked a whirlwind that we choose to see as Fourth of July fireworks.

We can be so out of touch with reality as a people only because we have failed to be meek, have refused to listen to the truth some artists and historians and religious leaders have tried to tell us about our past sins against American Indians, African slaves, and the people of the Philippines, Hiroshima and Nagasaki, Vietnam, Nicaragua, El Salvador, Grenada, and Panama. Our refusal to admit mistakes, issuing ultimatums rather than seeking negotiations, has more than once led us to the commission of war crimes that history will hold us accountable for. Only meekness, some modest acknowledgment of our rightful place as one member of a family of nations, can save us.

Everywhere, it can be seen what the absence of meekness has brought us to. A look at the suffering of the earth itself clarifies what Jesus meant when he said the meek shall inherit it. God first promised to Abraham "the earth," a new land, implicitly a place of rest and peace, a liveable place, the opposite of the increasingly violated planet we see around us. Today the earth chokes in the stranglehold that the violent and rapacious have on it. Jesus promised something else. If the earth survives, it will be because the meek have inherited it. Only they, because they know their true size in relation to the earth, can care for it appropriately.

The meek do not require that the earth serve them. They can collaborate with the earth as they collaborate with other people. The Aleutian peoples practiced meekness when they used every part of the whale that they killed and prayed for forgiveness before they killed it. Other Native Americans killed only enough buffalo to meet their needs. They taught their children to leave a camp site so undisturbed that no one could tell they had camped there, and they taught them how to be silent. Quietness is the environment of the meek. It does not terrify them with its emptiness; it embraces them in its fullness. It is a condition for the thoughtfulness that enables meekness.

Jesus' promise to the meek was not an inherited afterlife but an assurance of bliss on this earth because the earth will be good for their presence on it. The meek have the power to create goodness, for themselves and others. Their work is hard, their burden heavy, but their yoke—worn at the direction of their God—is light. Like the early Christians, they can't be put down. Because in one sense they already are "down," living close to the earth, not at the centers of power. But in a greater sense their power comes from elsewhere; they ultimately cannot lose. They are the "terrible meek" celebrated by author Flannery O'Connor and others who perceive that the most flawed personalities driven by the gospel can "inherit the land" and change it.

In O'Connor's story "The Artificial Nigger," an old man determined to impress his grandson with his knowledge of the big city, horrifies himself when he momentarily rejects the grandson. He is deeply grateful when the child forgives him. A prejudiced and stubborn man, he nevertheless grasps the implications of what he has done and is humble enough to ask for help. Returning from his one day in the city with his grandson, he reflects on the beauty of the world and his place in it:

> The moon, restored to its full splendor, sprang from a cloud and flooded the clearing with light. As they stepped off, the sage grass was shivering gently in shades of silver and the clinkers under their feet glittered with a fresh black light. The treetops, fencing the junction like the protecting walls of a garden, were darker than the sky which

was hung with gigantic white clouds illuminated like lanterns.

Mr. Head stood very still and felt the action of mercy touch him again but this time he knew that there were no words in the world that could name it. He understood that it grew out of agony, which is not denied to any man and which is given in strange ways to children. He understood it was all a man could carry into death to give his Maker and he suddenly burned with shame that he had so little of it to take with him. He stood appalled, judging himself with the thoroughness of God, while the action of mercy covered his pride like a flame and consumed it. He had never thought himself a great sinner before but he saw now that his true depravity had been hidden from him lest it cause him despair. He realized that he was forgiven for sins from the beginning of time, when he had conceived in his own heart the sin of Adam, until the present, when he had denied poor Nelson. He saw that no sin was too monstrous for him to claim as his own, and since God loved in proportion as He forgave, he felt ready at that instant to enter Paradise (O'Connor, pp. 269-270).

His pride having been consumed, Mr. Head becomes meek and knows the Paradise that earth can be.

The meek have power. It radiates from them. They make a difference in the land. Like Moses, they may not live to see the promised land, but they are not without the joys that come to those with confidence in God's promise. In *The Life of Moses*, Gregory of Nyssa describes the fading years of the meek leader who led his people across the desert to the edge of the promised land: the promise of the beatitude lives in the journey itself.

When you conquer all enemies (the Egyptian, the Amalekite, the Idumean, the Midianite), cross the water, are enlightened by the cloud, are sweetened by the wood, drink from the rock, taste of the food from above, make your ascent up the mountain through purity and sanctity; and when you arrive there, you are instructed in the divine mystery by the sound of the trumpets, and in the impenetrable darkness draw near to God by your faith. ...

Only poetry, like Gregory of Nyssa's or Flannery O'Connor's, can describe the joy of the meek, who seem to fail in human terms but do come to a habitable place, ascend the mountain of the Lord and draw near to God by faithful strategies that confound the world.

Inheriting the earth means living in the presence of God, whose earth it is. Once, worried about threats of violence to his young family, Martin Luther King was sitting at his kitchen table and experienced the presence of God telling him he would never be alone. Remembrance of that presence kept him faithful, not so much to a worthy cause as to God. Years later, as he spoke of his pain over the Vietnam War, he acknowledged that the war was not something he originally saw as part of his commitment to civil rights. Despite the counsel of his advisers that getting politically mired in criticism of the war would deflect energy and focus from civil rights, King felt he had to do it to be faithful. He said,

When I took up the cross, I recognized its meaning. ... The cross is something that you bear and ultimately that you die on. The cross may mean the death of your popularity. It may mean the death of a foundation grant. It may cut down your budget a little, but take up your cross, and just bear it. And that's the way I have decided to go (in Garrow, p. 564).

As a result of his faithfulness to the cross, his courage born of gentleness, before he died King inherited the earth. Like Moses, he came to the edge of the promised land, and ended with the promise of Jesus, as the bliss recorded in his final speech testifies:

Well, I don't know what will happen now. We've got some difficult days ahead. But it really doesn't matter with me now, because I've been to the mountaintop. And I don't mind. Like anybody, I would like to live a long life. Longevity has its place. But I'm not concerned about that now. I just want to do God's will. And he's allowed me to go up to the mountain, and I've looked over, and I've seen the promised land. I may not get there with you. But I want you to know tonight, that we, as a people will get to the promised land. And so I'm happy tonight. I'm not worried about anything. I'm not fearing any man. Mine eyes have seen the glory of the coming of the Lord.

4

Blessed Are They Who Hunger and Thirst for Justice

Where supermarkets and microwave ovens abound, it is not easy to know hunger and thirst, let alone hunger and thirst for a seeming abstraction like justice. Still, the beatitude "Blessed are they who hunger and thirst for justice; they shall be satisfied" loomed so large in the minds of those who recorded the words of Jesus that they elaborated on it further in the final one, "Blessed are they who suffer persecution for justice' sake. ..." The recorders knew that, for the person who lacks justice, it is far from abstract. It is an empty stomach, a weak body, a parched throat, a fever in the brain, feelings known to those who literally lack food and water.

The Greek New Testament translates the Hebrew *sedeq* (justice) with the root *dik* in the beatitudes. This root expresses more than "tit for tat" or the recognition that all must have roughly equal access to goods. The root *dik* includes these meanings but goes beyond them to express the fullness of right and happiness, the desire to see right prevail. It is often translated "righteousness," as in right relationship, but in contemporary parlance that word connotes an arrogance not associated with either the Greek *dikaiosyne* or the Hebrew *sedaquah.* In any case, the beatitude recalls the godly preoccupation iterated by the prophet Micah when he condenses God's command to its irreducible elements:

God has told you what is good;
and what is it that the Lord asks of you?
Only to act justly, to love loyalty,
to walk wisely before your God (Mi 6:8).

The magnitude of the quest for complete justice is underscored in the text by the imagery of hunger and thirst used to express the desire for it. If most of us, in a land of soft drink and candy machines, know little of real hunger, this was not true of Jesus' listeners, a crowd of working people akin to Latin American campesinos or Sri Lankan fishermen in their total dependence on the daily wage for their next meal. When gospel accounts say the apostles are mending their nets, fishing on the lake, and expressing chagrin at having fished all night and caught nothing, they are not describing avid sportsmen. The disciples' and their families' ability to eat depended on the catch. A working person in Palestine under the Roman occupation made barely enough to keep body together. Unable to work, one was reduced to begging, and likely to know hunger pangs.

We need water as much as food. Galilee is green and lovely, but three times a day women had to draw water from communal wells and carry it home for cooking, drinking, and washing. Slaking thirst was a labor-intensive task. One could swim in the sea of Galilee or wash in the Jordan River, but the sea was dangerous and the river neither wide nor accessible. Galilee was green, but much of Palestine was desert. Jesus' hearers may have walked up to Jerusalem for a feast or solemnity, perhaps using the Jericho road Jesus refers to familiarly in the parable of the Good Samaritan. Even today that road, though not through the country's worst desert, is a punishing day's walk in the sun, with the temperature in June at least 110° and few places for shade along the way.

Without water one could die merely walking from Jericho to Jerusalem.

Besides the relative scarcity of food and water for the people listening to Jesus, and their ability to make do with much less than we have, the Greek construction of the phrase "hunger for justice," according to Barclay, tells us that Jesus wishes his audience not to settle for half a loaf. Normally, the construction would use the genitive; that is, one would hunger for some bread, as the French say, "*du pain.*" In this instance, however, the Greek uses the accusative case, indicating the hungerer wants all of the bread, "the whole loaf."

In other words, we will be satisfied only when we hunger and thirst for the completion of justice, righteousness for all. In this regard, Jesus wants us to be like the figure of the Boddhisattva in Buddhism, who has achieved enlightenment himself but sacrifices it to labor among the rest of humankind until all arrive at freedom from suffering. Another model might be Eugene Debs, the great American socialist leader who said, "As long as one person is in prison, I am not free." Debs understood that poverty and injustice in a society create conditions that make crime, and hence prison, inevitable. His commitment to eliminate poverty and injustice would, in his view, eliminate the need for imprisonment. Both he and the Boddhisattva hungered for justice.

This beatitude shows us, perhaps more than any, the uncompromising nature of Jesus' view of what humankind both deserves and should desire. It is not the way of the world to want "the whole loaf" of justice, though the world does not deny to the privileged their "whole loaf" of power or prestige. Industrial magnates may, in the eyes of the world and of governments, be entitled to corner the market on a service or product. People admire them for making all the money they can make. Nations, too, may stake their claims to all the territory they can discover as long as they are big enough and martial enough to defend it. The history books may even applaud them for the boldness of their imperial adventures.

Although the great ones are considered great for taking as much power as they can, the little ones of the earth seek for justice and are counselled that achieving it is a gradual process. Justice can't be accomplished overnight, the world admonishes. And the world is correct. In fact, injustice has persisted for so long that it is the status quo, and those who would rectify it swim against a mighty current. It takes time and effort to educate people, to pry from a court the correct ruling and from the budget adequate money to address the problem even in a token way. Nevertheless, Jesus' response to this way of the world, I suspect, would echo the dictum, "Justice delayed is justice denied." Despite the world's advice to go slow at rectifying long-standing injustice, we must hunger for the whole loaf, and we must hunger for it now. We must be at least as wise as serpents who swallow whole the loaves of power.

For ten years I was the lobbyist at our state legislature for an ecumenical organization that took on the issues of the poor in the political forum and sought justice through changes in public policy. Through my work I came to know many of the poor people on whose behalf I lobbied. I often felt I had fallen into an unbridgeable chasm between the myriad needs of prisoners, migrant farmworkers, or mentally ill persons and the meager justice the officials were willing or able to dispense to them.

Most prisoners in our state are poor, undereducated, members of minority groups, people with small chance in our economic system. Justice requires, minimally, that we alter current economic dogmas that sacrifice too many to their idols. Also, common sense should prompt us to protect future victims of street crime by alleviating the harsh economic and social conditions that all but guarantee it. When jobs are scarce or low-paying and many persons lack the education for them, crime is a realistic option.

Legislators, however, rarely feel they have the luxury of taking this longer view. It is easier to get tough on crime by building prisons than by building schools, assuring health care, and improving the chances for jobs with adequate wages. It is easier to mollify voters by criminalizing ever more offenses and upping the ante with longer sentences every time the reported crime rate climbs higher.

In this political climate my job was to improve conditions for prisoners, to educate the public and legislators to the fact that much crime is a function of our economic system, and to work against harsher criminal penalties and for programs that would help people help themselves out of poverty. Mine was a worthy and difficult task, but it was not necessarily what Jesus was talking about in this beatitude. It assumed an incremental approach. I worked for a piece of the pie, *"du pain,"* some small signal that justice might appear on the horizon in our time. That work needs doing. It alleviates need and teaches patience and strategy.

But if more of us hungered for the whole loaf even as we worked for the crumbs, refusing to be satisfied with them, we would achieve justice with less delay. Congressman Paul Wellstone recently advised Hillary Rodham Clinton as she worked to put together a national health plan, "Don't be incremental—be bold." The mightier challenge may be to work incrementally without losing our boldness, compromising our vision. Unless we are emboldened, perhaps by desperation, unless we allow our boldness to overcome attachment to the usual, unless we recognize that we are a starving generation, our hunger and thirst will never be satisfied.

This beatitude also, with its emphasis on longing, the inner disposition of the hungerer, de-emphasizes behavior not born of deep desire. In his *Dictionary of the New Testament*, Leon-Dufour links it with Matthew 5:20 and Matthew 6:1, 33, contrasting those who "set their minds" on God's justice with those who "make a show of religion." The Pharisees and doctors of the law don't hunger. Their achievements are measured out in coffee spoons, as T. S. Eliot's Prufrock would say, deeds totalled up in clerical columns or counted by the commemorative plaques on the wall. For them, life is a

sequence of actions that progress in an orderly manner
toward some clear cut and rational goal that includes better-
ment of the human condition. Mere incrementalism again.
Those who live life this way are calm and articulate about
methodology and the distinction between strategies and tac-
tics, and long and short range goals. They do not apologize
that they have never pulled stars from the sky, have not been
able to bake and distribute the whole loaf.

The hungerer, on the other hand, is a dreamer, all
apologies and despair that the dream has not yet taken on
flesh. You can't tell her that she's come a long way because
she is consumed by the distance yet to be closed. The
hungerer is the mother of the child who has to walk five miles
to an inferior black school as white children pass by on a bus
bound for a nearby school with new books and a marching
band. He is the father of a little girl whose fourth grade
teacher encourages the boys to be doctors and the girls to be
nurses, and sends only boys to be tested for the gifted and
talented program. You can't tell these parents that their
children are better off today than a hundred years ago,
though that may be the fact of the matter. They are hungerers,
dreamers who say with John F. Kennedy: "Some people see
things as they are and ask why; I see them as they could be
and ask why not?"

The hungerer also dreams with Martin Luther King, who
in his speech at the 1963 March on Washington described his
dream in such tangible terms as to make others ache for it as
he did:

> I have a dream that one day on the red hills of
> Georgia, the sons of former slaves and the sons of
> former slave owners will be able to sit down
> together at the table of brotherhood.
>
> I have a dream that one day, even the state of
> Mississippi, a state sweltering with the heat of
> injustice, will be transformed into an oasis of
> freedom and justice.

> I have a dream that my four little children will one day live in a nation where they will not be judged by the color of their skin but by the content of their character. I have a dream today (in Garrow, pp. 283-284)!

Although less concrete than Martin Luther King in his use of language, Pope Paul VI in his 1971 encyclical *Octogesima Adveniens*, also speaks of hungering when he describes the need for utopian visions. Acknowledging the dangers of utopias as convenient excuses for those who "wish to escape from concrete tasks in order to take refuge in an imaginary world," he notes nonetheless that utopias can provoke the imagination both "to perceive in the present the disregarded possibility hidden within it" and to impel into the future.

> The Spirit of the Lord, who animates man renewed in Christ, continually breaks down the horizons within which his understanding likes to find security and the limits to which his activity would willingly restrict itself; there dwells within him a power which urges him to go beyond every system and every ideology (*Octogesima Adveniens*).

Beyond every system and ideology is the place where only they who hunger for the whole loaf and thirst for the fountain of life can go.

The opposite of hungering is settling. You may see the injustice as clearly and suffer from it as much as anyone, but circumstances compel you to work hard and accept the measure of food and drink you can get to sustain yourself and this generation. Perhaps that mere sustenance keeps you at near-starvation levels, but at least you are surviving and can hope that the future will bring more opportunity for justice. You can deal with the present only as it is. You have "settled."

Idealistic youth often perceive their elders as having settled. They think them complacent and complicit with injustice. Youth hunger and thirst even though (and perhaps because) they have not yet experienced the obstacles to satisfaction their elders warn them of and try to prepare them for. Outsiders often accuse others who have achieved insider status of having settled, of hungering no more. I once worked with some black teachers who told their black students, "I got mine; you get yours." The students thought the teachers had settled in the worst way.

A talented friend told me that after she had climbed to the upper executive reaches of a large corporation, she realized that she had developed some "male-coping mechanisms" in order to do so. Now I think of her phrase whenever I feel the clericalism of some women clergy and officiousness of some black bureaucrats. Developing coping mechanisms enabled them to achieve their personal goals, to alleviate their own hunger, but the mechanisms took them over. They lost their vision of the whole. Perhaps because they had to move alone into hostile arenas, their hunger for the whole loaf of justice was blunted. They settled for a separate peace, ate a piece of bread, sipped at water not yet proffered to those on the outside. Now they no longer hunger. But also they are not satisfied.

The characters Creon and Antigone in Sophocles' play *Antigone* personify the "settler" and the "hungerer." Antigone's brother, killed leading a rebellion, was left unburied outside the city. Defying the ruler Creon's edict, Antigone scatters dirt on her brother's body, which—according to the gods' laws--must be buried. For this action, Antigone eventually loses her own life. She cannot accede to Creon's opinion that human decrees can sometimes supercede the unwritten and eternal laws.

Creon is no evil man, merely one who has inherited the task of restoring order after an era of civic turbulence. He considers Antigone rash and headstrong but only reluctantly punishes her for her deed. He is understandably preoccupied with order, telling the people:

Our city has been tossed
By a tempestuous ocean, but the gods
Have steadied it once more and made it safe.

He puts regard for the city before personal loyalties because he believes that only the stability of the state makes more intimate relations possible. Antigone dies because she believes that human law must bow to the divine. Creon's law, she says

Was not proclaimed by Zeus,
Or by the gods who rule the world below.
I do not think your edicts have such power
That they can override the laws of heaven,
Unwritten and unfailing, laws whose life
Belongs not to today or yesterday
But to time everlasting.

Antigone is foolish in the eyes of the world, as her sister Ismene and the Greek Chorus remind us; her brother did, after all, kill his own brother and lead a foreign army against his own city. He was no hero. But for Antigone, a hungerer, these are peripheral considerations. The central one is righteousness. Creon, the moderate and responsible settler, uses graceful analogies to argue against rigidity:

You have seen
Trees on the margin of a stream in winter:
Those yielding to the flood save every twig,
And those resisting perish root and branch.

By implication, Antigone is the doomed and graceless resister. But the prophet Tiresias supports Antigone, who goes to her death asking, "What is the law of heaven I have broken?"

Sophocles' play illustrates Jesus' saying, "Blessed are they who hunger and thirst for justice." It calls to mind generation after generation of persons who stand up to the prevailing powers to claim the right of conscience. During World War II the French playwright Jean Anouilh rewrote

Sophocles' play to show Creon as the practical and wise man whose advice would lead the French to collaborate with the Vichy government, the Nazi regime in France. Anouilh's Antigone vigorously asserts principle over the easy ways of everyday, and, in so doing, portrays the hungerer. Accused by her sister of not caring enough about life to want to go on living, Antigone exclaims:

> Go on living! Who was it that was always the first out of bed because she loved the touch of the cold morning air on her bare skin? Who was always the last to bed because nothing less than infinite weariness could wean her from the lingering night? Who wept when she was little because there were too many grasses in the meadow, too many creatures in the field, for her to know and touch them all?

Some might describe Antigone as a mere romantic, but she accepts the real consequences of her decisions. In Anouilh's play she explodes to Creon:

> I spit on your idea of life—that life must go on, come what may. You are all like dogs that lick everything they smell. You with your promise of humdrum happiness—provided a person doesn't ask too much of life. I want everything of life, I do; and I want it now! I want it total, complete: otherwise I reject it! I will *not* be moderate. I will *not* be satisfied with the bit of cake you offer me if I promise to be a good little girl.

Antigone hungers for the whole loaf.

Unlike Creon and other "settlers," both Sophocles' and Anouilh's Antigones are hungerers. So are Franz Jagerstatter, Rosa Parks, Daniel Berrigan, and many others. Though they may have spent much of their lives about the ordinary tasks of making a home, tending the sick, teaching the next generation, they recognize the moment in which they must drink of the cup, grasp at the whole loaf of justice, before it recedes from their reach once again. They stand up for God's justice over merely human law, and they stand firm. They show in their lives the insistent pangs of real hunger and the persistent thirst that Jesus blesses through the beatitude.

But how are they satisfied? As I write, millions starve in the Horn of Africa where three of the last four years have brought no rain. Hurricanes in Panama and Costa Rica and a major cyclone in Bangladesh have knocked out of our headlines the Kurds freezing on Turkish mountainsides. Nature and humankind seem to conspire in injustice against the poor of the world, those most exposed to the elements and most likely to be refugees from bombs. They bleed, hunger, and thirst for food, water, and justice. What is their satisfaction?

Jesus promised to the hungerer neither a rose garden here and now, nor pie in the sky by and by. But no one who has lived in proximity to those who hunger for righteousness can doubt that for them, no matter what the external circumstances, life is richer and more intense than for those who do not so hunger. They take the ingredients for despair and cook up a passionate meal on the open flame of hope. They hunger and thirst because they believe that food and drink are at hand, will arrive, no matter the objective evidence, the closed roads, bridges washed out, or brigands at the curves. And their hope makes more possible the coming of food, the advent of justice. Their faith in the midst of calamity, while others depend on the facts, renders more possible the surprise they await.

I know an old woman who has known a lot of trouble. She lived more than half her life under Jim Crow laws in the South, worked as a cook and eventually as a teacher's aide. She married a man with a weakness for alcohol who lived in a culture that drove even stronger men to alcohol. They adopted two bright and sensitive youngsters, both of whom became drug addicts, one of them while doing his tour of duty in Vietnam. She worked and she prayed; she prayed and she worked. But life was hard. Although not eloquent, she grasped the nature of her suffering and wrestled with it. A pious woman, she would nonetheless occasionally let slip a remark that showed she knew her pain was not God-ordained but rooted in the injustice of a society that disregards the black and poor.

One sweltering day I arrived at her house as she came home wearing a pretty but rumpled dress, an exquisite hat, and white gloves! She was breathless and perspiring from a tight girdle, and her swollen feet escaped the edges of her shoes. It was a weekday, so I assumed she had come from a funeral. Only a funeral could elicit a get-up like that on a day like this, I thought. But no, she had gone to lunch with a group of retired teachers' aides at the Tara Inn, a fancy country club restaurant north of town. It wasn't a place I expected her to go or to be able to afford. A lunch at the Tara Inn could cost her a trip to the supermarket.

My face must have shown my mind's question, because she answered it. "I don't really like that place," she said, "but I sure enjoyed going. Until just a year ago they never let black folks in their front door, and now they have to. They ran the place with black maids and gardeners and caddies all those years. I just wanted to take my black body there once to get waited on, and now I'm satisfied. I was eating for a lot of folks." She collapsed onto a chair, pulled off her shoes, and grinned. Her lunch at the Tara was, in her words, "a taste of heaven"—not a single meal but recompense for decades of hunger for justice. This evening or tomorrow might be fractured, but this noon was whole, satisfying. She would celebrate it for a long time.

A friend who labored for peace through many seemingly fruitless years told me that at the birth of his first grandchild he thought he might despair because he realized that the world she was coming into was even more tortured than the one to which he had been born. Despite that premonition, when he actually held the baby for the first time, his whole body pulsed with the sense that this was the child who could make the difference, that indeed every child could. He was for the first time satisfied that peace is possible, assured that it is not too late, and his thought and work are now suffused with new surety. I feel it in him. I also believe that his own hunger for peace, when presented with the child, generated his sense of satisfaction.

Others tell of being in the presence of great people who communicate satisfaction even in the midst of their hunger. Oscar Romero, Caesar Chavez, Desmond Tutu, and Dorothy Day are among the better known. Bishop Tutu was once asked by an interviewer, "In what do you hope?" He responded that he didn't have the luxury of hope because the daily reality in South Africa was so critical that he could only apply himself entirely to each situation as it arose. Nevertheless he laughs a lot, a rich and effervescent laugh. His humor, often drawing on the ridiculous disparity between what is and what could be, illustrates both his hunger and his joy in the moment.

Saint Augustine says, "Thou hast made us for thyself, O Lord, and our hearts are restless till they rest in thee." "Are hungry till they feed on thee," we might add. Thomas Aquinas writes that we always seek—hunger for—the good, which is God. Even those who pursue evil, pursue it because they mistakenly think it good. But the only satisfied ones are those who find the real good, seize it, and consume it—eat God. Evil is not a fulfilling meal, nor are phantasms. Only real bread, eaten with a sense of its holiness, fills us. Only real drink, from an oasis, not a mirage, quenches our thirst. And only the really hungry and thirsty know the difference.

If we don't thirst deeply, it hardly matters that the water is a mirage. We won't be satisfied, merely puzzled. If we don't hunger greatly, it doesn't matter that they feed us Cool Whip instead of bread and butter. We can go through the motions, keep the external observance of eating and drinking, barely noticing what we've eaten. Neither thirsting nor hungering, we live in a limbo of constantly shifting, vaguely comprehended desires. Only those who hunger—steadily, starvingly—can ever be satisfied.

5

Blessed Are the Merciful

"This country is going to the dogs, so I will never vote against capital punishment," barked one usually thoughtful state legislator explaining to me his refusal to vote to exempt mentally handicapped persons from the death penalty. "This country is going to the dogs; we need more spanking of children," shouted another to justify his vote against allowing some school districts to refrain from using corporal punishment.

In our country punishment is a way of life. U.S. prisons hold proportionately more people than those of any other industrialized nation. What most of those people have in common is dark skin, poverty, and lack of those skills needed to make their way in a work-oriented technocratic culture. They are an underclass for the most part, further punished by prison for already being poor. On local and national levels, when we are frustrated by persistent poverty or other problems, we punish someone. On the international level as well, we go after leaders with names like Gadhafi, Khomeini, Saddam, Ortega, or Noriega and are none too careful about how many innocent people we maim, kill, or render homeless in the process.

Mercy would have none of this. The Hebrew word *hesed* urges us not to get the skin of the others but to get inside their skin. The beatitude, "Blessed are the merciful," urges that our attitudes and behavior toward others be motivated by empathy, an ability to feel with them and see things from their perspective. The Spanish call persons with this ability *simpatico*, and it is a compliment. Empathy means more than mere sympathy and certainly more than pity. The Greek translation of this beatitude uses *eleemon*, the root of our word for almsgiving, which fails to communicate the depth of identification with the other that *hesed* does. "Empathy" is closer to *hesed*.

"Compassion," with its Latin root, is like "empathy," derived from the Greek. Significantly compassion is the common goal of the world's major religions. The Hindu god Ramakrishna howled with pain as he watched two boatmen quarrelling angrily; he so identified with their sorrows and with those of the whole world. The eminently rational Buddha balanced his critical objectivity with a tenderness that made him risk his life to rescue a goat caught on mountain brambles. The Zen poet Seng Ts'an writes that to trust in the heart is to be "not two." Becoming one with the other embodies the ultimate in empathy.

Call it monism if you will, but in the East there is a bias toward subjective interaction that the rational West has a difficult time apprehending. When Mount Everest was first scaled, Western writers spoke of the "conquest of Everest." In his *The Religions of Man*, Huston Smith tells of the Oriental writer influenced by Taoism who said it should be considered rather "the befriending of Everest." To the compassionate, even the mountain is not a thing but a kindred being.

The great Confucian Mo Tzu wrote nearly five hundred years before Christ that human evil in the world would fade when one regards

> the state of others as one's own, the houses of others as one's own, the persons of others as one's self. ... When all the people in the world love one

another, then the strong will not overpower the
weak, the many will not oppress the few, the wealthy will not mock the poor, the honored will not
disdain the humble, and the cunning will not
deceive the simple (in Smith, p. 173).

For the Confucian, empathy is the key to justice as well
as mercy.

The East may have mined the nonrational or heart origins
of compassion more deeply than the West, but the "Religions
of the Book" know it as well. In eminently practical Islam,
compassion is institutionalized in the requirement that each
year each Muslim must give one-fortieth of income and
holdings to the poor. Judaism's perspective is the lesson of
the Exile, vicarious suffering, whereby a believer accepts
"pain in order that others may be spared it" (Smith, p. 280).
In neither of these religions is God more punitive than loving.
They ask humankind to be the same.

The sign of Christianity since apostolic times has been
"how they love one another" because they are all part of the
same body. The traditional doctrine of the Mystical Body of
Christ, elaborated from Jesus' words, "I am the vine and you
are the branches," inspired Saint Paul. In his discourse to the
Romans Paul says: "For just as in a single human body there
are many limbs and organs ... so all of us, united with Christ,
form one body, serving individually as limbs and organs to
one another" (Rom 12:4-5). The sacrament of the eucharist
acts as both reminder and re-enactment of that union with
Christ's body.

Consequently, we show mercy one to another because we
are all members of the same body, sons and daughters of the
same Father, our brother Jesus having been incarnated to
oneness with our flesh and to death in the ultimate act of
mercy. In his encyclical *Rich in Mercy*, Pope John Paul II writes
that the beatitude "Blessed are the merciful, for they shall
obtain mercy" is "the synthesis of the whole of the good
news, of the 'wonderful exchange' contained therein." This
beatitude, he continues, contains the truth of God in Christ,

who enables us to "see him as particularly close to man, especially when man is suffering, when he is under threat at the very heart of his existence and dignity." In this sense, mercy is God's response to the poor in spirit. In mercy God comes very close; in mercy we come close to one another.

The practical application of the merciful attitude based on "exchange" or feeling with another is forgiveness. "To understand is to forgive" goes the saying. Many gospel parables—the Lost Sheep, the Good Samaritan, the Merciless Servant among them—exemplify the deed of forgiveness flowing from compassion. John Paul II in *Rich in Mercy* dwells on the parable of the Prodigal Son. The erring son hopes only to be taken back as an employee in his father's house; he expects mere justice. His father, however, exemplifies *hesed* and will have nothing less than full reinstatement of his son and a party to celebrate it. The father "had compassion, ran to meet him, threw his arms around his neck and kissed him," says John Paul II. "His heart went out to him," says Luke (15:20).

Mercy is the fulfillment of justice. It requires justice as a minimum. If justice is not already present or implicit in the mercy I would bring, then the latter is mere show. I can hardly say "I forgive you" to my sister when I have been the offender. The victim must forgive, though the best route for mercy may be a two-way street where victim and offender approach each other with open arms.

St. Vincent de Paul, referring to the dangers of charitable giving, says,

> You will find out that charity
> Is a heavy burden to carry,
> Heavier than the bowl of soup
> And the full basket. ...
> It is only for your love alone
> That the poor will forgive you
> The bread you give to them.

Charities born of mere kindness (with only a nod toward justice) don't survive for long as effective helping instruments; recipients of such charity inevitably exert their autonomy, perhaps through passive aggression, often a refusal to keep the charity's rules. Then the donors become impatient, or at least bemused, by recipients who fail to demonstrate gratitude. The real offenders, however, are donors who scatter alms from a lofty perch rather than the playing field they are hoping to level. Theirs is *noblesse obliqe*, a decidedly pagan virtue.

Even the pagans, however, learned the practical value of the deed of forgiveness. It simply allows life to go on. Twenty-five hundred years ago the Greek dramatist Aeschylus, celebrated as the triumph of wisdom, humankind's movement beyond revenge to forgiveness. In his *Oresteia*, each in a series of royal murderers intends his or her blow to stop the generations of bloodfeud, but revenge takes on a life of its own and seemingly cannot be stopped. Disturbed by the bloody behavior of the humans, some gods urge vengeance, but the goddess Athena intervenes. The Furies argue against compassion: "Should this be, every man will find a way to act at his own caprice." But Athena teaches, contrarily, that the people will be decimated and the land destroyed unless someone forgives. The rational Greeks chose to learn from her that mercy serves self-interest by ensuring survival. Tit for tat results in the end of all.

Mercy may not always seem reasonable, however. The prodigal son's brother, who stayed home, resents what he perceives as rewarding his brother's frivolity. There is no welcome-home party, he whines, for the one who has never abandoned his father's house. "No free lunch" is the comparable cry of many Americans who object to assistance for brothers and sisters at home and abroad. Both public officials and private foundations hear that cry and try to assure that only the deserving poor get help. Consequently, they harness their workers with restrictions and paperwork that let many poor people free fall through so-called safety nets. Thus reason evicts efficacy and mercy at once.

Dorothy Day used to tell her Catholic Worker colleagues not to distinguish between the deserving and undeserving poor because even governments eventually get around to assisting the former. Officials consume resources, however, in the process of making sure that "welfare queens" and other "ineligibles" do not scale the paperwork walls. Guardians against the undeserving are the stay-at-home brothers who hope to secure the world against prodigal fathers. Mercy, meanwhile, does not distinguish between deserving and undeserving, because in the eyes of God we are all both.

Sometimes mercy is the only justice. Since reinstatement of the death penalty ten years ago, our state has executed three criminals. On the days they died, local newspapers printed their life stories. All three were born into poverty, unwanted by parents who abused them unspeakably. Mentally, emotionally, or physically handicapped, they were rejected by all they met, their pilgrimage from birth to death row seemingly unrelieved by joy. They struck back with horrible violence toward others. In their clumsy duel of cruelties with the human community they knew, the final thrust was capital punishment. Killing the killers ended the problem that was their lives.

But what the state called justice was no more than a dead end for three souls to whom mercy might have extended some compensation for the cruelty to which they were born. Mercy cannot remedy the deaths of earlier victims, but we fool ourselves in thinking another murder can. When we execute a person, we merely close the circle of victimization that only forgiveness can break open. Even that pagan Aeschylus knew this.

One reason we find mercy or compassion hard to practice is our inability to listen well, to hear what flows deep within another's heart. Most have experienced the refreshment of feeling truly heard by another. The presence of a genuine listener renews us. Jesus counsels, "Let the one who has ears to hear, hear." Liturgical petitions ask God to "incline an ear" and "hear our prayer." Jesus' friend Martha was kind, serious about ministering to his and the disciples' needs. But her busyness evokes the image of the overworked woman in modern ministry who sets up the chairs, runs off the programs, leads the music, visits the hospitals, and teaches the marriage preparation course. Every parish has at least one such woman. Unlike Martha, her sister Mary chose to put aside her tasks and listen to the Lord. Mary was *simpatico*. Listening was her prayer, in fact, and Jesus honored it above Martha's busyness.

The whole world needs a listening ear like Mary's. One of my images of peace is half the world listening to the other half all morning, and then reversing their positions in the afternoon. I have travelled to Central America and the Middle East to visit with distraught communities living where bombs had just fallen and were likely to fall again at any moment. People in these communities rejoiced that we brought food and medicine or helped them get in their crops or rebuild their houses, but what they preferred was sitting over a glass of tea or a cup of cold water with us and telling their stories. Their parting injunctions often were, "Go home and tell people who we are. We want a future for our children. We want peace." Their requests echoed the need expressed by Shakespeare's dying tragic characters who beg their listeners to "tell my story and tell it right."

Human beings long to be heard because true hearing constitutes understanding. Failure to be heard leads to frustration, even violence to oneself or others. Whole classes of people rise up against those who fail or refuse to hear them. Once in Bolivia an incident confirmed that truth for me.

Standoff

We round the bend from Titikaka
to brake for a boy and man in rags.
The elder squints toward the windshield

and brandishes two skull size rocks
gouged from the road.

The child at my window wants money.
For clearing the road of rocks?
Hurling one away from us
in prophecy of shattered glass,
the man holds high the other.

Our driver inches the jeep ahead,
its hood to the man's hat held out
like begging bowl, holey as sieve:
hat in one hand, rock in the other,
entreaty weighted with promise.

We sit for an eternal minute.

At last another car arrives.
Faces fusing outrage and relief,
man and boy fade into the cliff face,
half the world longing
to be heard by the other half.

In her *Despair and Personal Power in the Nuclear Age*,
Buddhist psychologist Joanna Macy credits a woman named
Frances Peavey as the "bravest listener" she knows. Peavey
travelled the world to find out what ordinary people think
of the prospects for our planet. In Tokyo, Bangkok, and Delhi
she sat on a bench in a central square, a sign set up beside her
reading "American Willing to Listen." Although she told
them she was merely an ordinary citizen, people lined up to
talk to her all day and into the night. And she took notes.

In Delhi she met the representative from Tonga attending
a conference of nonaligned nations. He found a table for
Peavey in the lobby of the hotel where the conference was
being held. One delegate after another came to talk to her,
and be listened to. The readiness of many to collaborate in
Peavey's listening project may indicate how rarely people
feel heard, especially by those they think have power to affect
their world.

Nature today both illustrates our failure to show mercy and offers us an opportunity to learn how. Because humans have "dominion" over the natural world, we lord it over her. We often empathize less with nature than with our fellow humans. We cannot accuse her of ill will or aggression toward us, and yet we make war on her in multitudinous ways. Much of our technology demands it. Our dying oceans and air testify to it.

Geologian Thomas Berry speaks of our autism with respect to the natural world. Every time a species dies, one more voice is silenced. We then hear less, are cut off from more. Gradually we sever connections with many voices. Eventually we will live alone, no longer able to perform the specifically human function of reflecting on the glory of creation. We will become autistic. Our self-absorption will have detached us from all reality but ourselves. All empathy, compassion, embodiment in the mystical Body of Christ stands at risk before our cutting off the voices of nature. Even our religious symbols lose meaning when we neglect mercy: how can we, Berry asks, baptize with polluted water?

Listening to nature and learning to feel with her works like an antidote to our arrogance. It softens our stiffness toward the world. In Shakespeare's play, only when the stubborn King Lear stands on the heath and submits himself to the raging tempest, does he hear the Fool, symbol of truth, and begin to feel the human condition:

> Poor naked wretches, wheresoe'er you are,
> That bide the pelting of this pitiless storm,
> How shall your houseless heads and unfed sides,
> Your loop'd and window'd raggedness, defend you
> From seasons such as these? O, I have ta'en
> Too little care of this! Take physic, pomp;
> Expose yourself to feel what wretches feel,
> That thou mayst shake the superflux to them
> And show the heavens more just (III iv 28-36).

Lear hears, experiences empathy with naked wretches, and commits himself to be more merciful in order to show forth the justice of heaven.

Francis of Assisi's profound empathy or communion with nature was as total as his compassion for humankind, especially the poor. In *The Brothers Karamazov* Father Zossima says of the Francis-like, gentle Alyosha,

> My young brother asks forgiveness of the birds. It may seem absurd, but it is right nonetheless for everything, like the ocean, flows and comes into contact with everything else. Touch it in one place and it reverberates at the other end of the world.

Here Zossima unwittingly describes a proposition of chaos theory, that discipline of physics that studies the non-linear behavior of systems. Chaos theorists propose that the flutter of a butterfly's wing can eventuate in a hurricane halfway round the world, so interconnected are the events of the universe. When the beatitudes bless mercy, it seems, they hallow the oneness among beings that science now discovers. In other words, the Mystical Body of Christ is now shown to be more than a mere metaphor for relationships.

The examples of Lear and St. Francis do not argue that we should use the natural world to learn compassion for the human. We have used nature enough. Rather, nature is part of the body of God, our own body, to which we must show mercy in order to complete mercy. Nonhuman nature, being nonrational, may give us our best chance to practice mercy, a movement of heart more than head. In Annie Dillard's *Holy the Firm*, a burning moth, a burning child, a burning nun, and a burning god shade into one another. Dillard's poetic prose, nonrational truth, tells us, "The god of today is a tree. He is a forest of trees or a desert, or a wedge from wideness down to a scatter of stars, stars like salt low and dumb and abiding" (Dillard, p. 62).

And each part of the world reflects the other, as it all reflects God: "It is starting to utter its infinite particulars, each overlapping and lone, like a hundred hills of hounds all giving tongue. ... Above me the mountains are raw nerves, sensible and exultant, held in a greeting or glance fully formed" (Dillard, p. 65). If we can vibrate along with the raw nerves of the world, through compassion, we can also slip into the human other and into God. Insofar as we fail to feel with nature, however, we fail to enter into God and relate to one another.

Many people are uncomfortable with animals. They consider cats sneaky, dogs fawning, insects made for squishing, and larger creatures potential beasts of burden. Others treat pets like spoiled children, feeding them too much, buying silly clothes and toys for them, filling up conversations with them as doting grandparents do with grandchildren. Both sorts of people judge and value animals by human standards and needs. In actuality, animals represent alternative modes of knowing the world. Dogs hear what we cannot, birds of prey see through angles of vision we lack, and cats preserve wildness in the midst of domestic life. Both those who mistrust animals and those who pamper them lack understanding and compassion for them.

Animals are the other and shall not be measured by the human, though humans can learn from them. In *The Outermost House*, Henry Beston ponders the connection between animals and humans and opines that they live by different voices. Animals "are not brethren; they are not underlings; they are other nations, caught with ourselves in the net of life and time, fellow prisoners of the splendour and travail of the earth" (Beston, p. 25). Accepting that animals are "other nations" may help us abjure dominion over them. Letting go of the casual mastery of them we have accustomed ourselves to can be an act of empathy, for some a step in letting go of attempts to master other humans. Empathy demands forsaking dominion.

At this moment I can hear giant earth movers in the woods below my house. They are felling all the trees in a forty-foot swathe that bounds a creek dammed by beaver.

The earth movers' goal is a sewer line designed to serve a small shopping center with its own fast food outlet at one end and a community with failed septic tanks at the other. The men and the machines ravish everything in their path and leave behind them uprooted old trees, litter from their lunches, and compacted soil where they have moved and piled pipes and stone. In the month since they arrived, quiet has fled from these woods.

Even worse, the wildlife has fled. I no longer hear the plop of beavers' tails as they warn one another of danger. The great blue herons don't sit on the stumps and greet the morning with their immobile praise, and the fierce crack of their voices no longer pierces the dusk. The ducks who wove in and out of the swamp's eddies are gone, as are the small birds who fed on the branches at its margins. I no longer see foxes and deer coming to drink at the stream.

I try to speak to the authorities about the way they are building this sewer, but the men hear merely complaint, a woman opposed to progress, denying their right to work or the rights of people who need a sewer. I fail to make my point. I want them to build a sewer gently. To take down trees with loving hands, use quiet machines or none, dig ditches carefully so that the creatures who live next to them will not be terrorized into flight. I wonder, in this county filling up with people, where the animals will go.

When the sewer is finished, I hope the deer and the birds will return. I long to hear the great blue heron's crotchety call again, to see her sitting on a rotting trunk drinking in the new day's mist. I have my doubts. Meanwhile, I wonder whether we can learn—before it is too late—to live without displacing others. Can we move in mental moccasins, quiet as the native peoples who came before us, so that we might have the necessary sewers and our fellow animal nations as well? Can we learn to show them mercy? Recognize that they do not exist only to serve our needs?

Mercy flows from compassion; it demands a subjective relationship with another in which the two can feel as one. It does not deny their "two-ness," disrespect the differences. It does enable the union of equals, genuine others, not superiors and inferiors. On the one hand modern science, the new physics for example, confirms for us the interrelatedness of beings in the world. On the other hand, it tends also to put forth a mechanistic view of nature based on a mathematical tradition stretching back to Plato. In her book *The Death of Nature*, Carolyn Merchant concludes that this latter view remains ascendant in modern science. To the extent that it is objective and "value-free," searching for ultimate unifying particles like quarks, science reduces all behavior to the quantifiable. It does not allow a thing—or a person—to be more than the sum of its parts.

This materialism looks upon an object but fails to hear the subject. It results in the degradation of nature and of the quality of life for all, but especially for those most identified with nature and natural processes, women bound by biology and native peoples traditionally living close to the earth. It is no accident that the rule of humankind over nature in the modern world coincides with the rule of white males over the entire globe and its peoples.

Physicist Brian Swimme, whose ancestry is Native American, thinks that we live today with the most constricted view of the human ever, largely because we have a limited understanding of the cosmos. Our merciless rape of the earth and entire peoples arises from failure to feel our connection with the earth and our ultimate oneness with others. The science of ecology addresses this failure by teaching holism, not a new understanding but a new sense of the interconnectedness we have largely forgotten. "No element of an interlocking cycle can be removed without the collapse of the cycle. The parts themselves take their meaning from the whole," writes Merchant. Here, she obliquely describes the Mystical Body of Christ, the theological reason for mercy. In both theological and ecological terms, we must feel with the other or we cease to feel anything.

From capital punishment to ecological sensitivity, we may seem to have ranged far in the discussion of "Blessed are the merciful ... ." But the beatitudes are such that once you begin to ponder them, you are in for an eye opening ride. They carry us to their deepest meaning, which is the good of the universe.

But what is the good of mercy? What does it mean to "obtain mercy," to eat the fruit of this beatitude in our time? It is to live as though forgiven for an unspeakable crime, which was then completely forgotten as well. It is to be blessed by pardon and amnesia at once. To live a less constricted life, as though after decades to move out of a house of thin-minded people who pass unflinching judgment on one's every movement from narrow gray room to narrow gray room. To become the human equivalent of the "finished and complete" animal Beston describes. Completed by the mercy of Jesus, we pass beyond judgment.

Yes, there is judgment in Christianity. We have saints and sinners, sheep and goats, the right hand and the left. But all can show mercy, and be shown it. The judgment meted out to the merciful is like the judgment of the birds anthropologist Loren Eisley observes in *The Star Thrower*. In a forest clearing Eisley came on an enormous raven with a squirming nestling in its beak. The nestling's parents cried and flew helplessly in the face of the larger bird's indifference. Into the clearing also came various small birds drawn by the parents' cries. None dared attack the larger raven, but they all cried in

> some instinctive common misery, the bereaved and the unbereaved. The glade filled with their soft rustling and their cries. They fluttered as though to point their wings at the murderer. There was a dim intangible ethic he had violated, that they knew. He was a bird of death (Eisley, p. 9).

But, Eisley concludes, the judgment did not end there. Although the raven continued unperturbed, the song of the birds changed.

> For in the midst of protest, they forgot the violence. There, in that clearing, the crystal note of a song sparrow lifted hesitantly in the hush. And finally, after painful fluttering, another took the song, and then another, the song passing from one bird to another, doubtfully at first, as though some evil thing were slowly forgotten. Till suddenly they took heart and sang from many throats joyously together as birds are known to sing. They sang because life is sweet and sunlight beautiful. They sang under the brooding shadow of the raven. In simple truth they had forgotten the raven, for they were the singers of life, and not of death (Eisley, p. 9).

The birds show the promise of the beatitudes, singing joy in the midst of sorrow. In giving mercy we too receive mercy's relief, freedom from the constrictions of life lived by calculation rather than empathy. Like the birds, we move beyond death. How must the father of the prodigal son have felt when he saw his son coming on the path? As young again as a child who gets the perfect red wagon for Christmas, as joyful as the mother who has just given birth. The returning son is mercy itself that the father receives for being merciful. The act redounds upon the actor. No greater lightness of being exists than in the act of forgiving, the giving over of the weight of judgment that compacts the soul as earthmoving equipment compacts the soil. Mercy means breathing again.

Nature blesses those who offer mercy to her. Jane Goodall has worked thirty years to save chimpanzees, a rapidly diminishing species, because she cares for them. In *Through a Window*, she writes about a gift received from the forest one day in the pale sunshine after a rain:

> The air was filled with a feathered symphony, the evensong of birds. I heard new frequencies in their

music and, too, in the singing of insect voices, notes
so high and sweet that I was amazed. I was intensely aware of the shape, the colour of individual
leaves, the varied patterns of the veins that made
each one unique. Scents were clear, easily identifiable—fermenting, overripe fruit; water-logged
earth; cold, wet bark; the damp odour of chimpan-
zee hair and, yes, my own too. And the aromatic
scent of young, crushed leaves was almost over-
powering. I sensed the presence of a bushbuck,
then saw him, quietly browsing upwind, his
spiralled horns dark with rain. And I was utterly
filled with that peace "which passeth all understanding" (Goodall, p. 67).

Later, as she crouched over her cooking fire, Goodall
realized she may have been experiencing the world as chimpanzees do. She concludes that humans would gain from that
perspective. She and Loren Eisley are among those who have
learned from the natural world the practice of compassion.
They are qualified to describe the peace of those who obtain
mercy as a consequence of their practice of it.

Most of us seek and obtain mercy mainly in the human
community. That blesses us also. The Russian Orthodox say,
"A person can be damned alone but can only be saved with
others." Community happens when we want to share ourselves and all we have. We give till it hurts, and we are sure
to be hurt. But hurt always arrives bearing an invitation to
join in the round of forgiving and being forgiven. If we don't
join in, we cut ourselves off from the community, one member at a time perhaps, one child, one parent, one friend, one
animal, one tree.

A growing body of research indicates that showing
mercy even has physical benefits. The immune system
responds to a person's attitudes. One study presented at a
1992 conference on brain research at the University of
California at San Diego investigated the effect of thoughts on
the body. An anxious thought, it found, changes the pH factor

of saliva that regulates the amount of adrenalin released to nerves and muscles. Refusal to forgive, a clinging to past hurts, can be a source of anxiety and consequently of bodily dysfunction. Thus forgiving persons are merciful not only to others but also to their own bodies. They receive the mercy they dispense.

Either we live to forgive, to show mercy, or we live to punish. And punishment constricts us. Our corporal and capital punishments, our prison populations and polluted air judge us, separate us from others and our own well-being. But when we cease punishing, stop judging, when we forgive and give and share, we lighten our own burdens and others'. Then we empathize with and can hear the voices of many others. We know community. We live in mercy.

Happy is the [person] who does not ...
take [a] seat among the scornful. ...
[This person] is like a tree
planted beside a watercourse
which yields its fruit in season
and its leaf never withers:
in all that he does he prospers (Ps 1:1, 3).

6

Blessed Are the Pure of Heart

Anticipating martyrdom, St. Thomas a Becket in T.S. Eliot's play, *Murder in the Cathedral*, says:

> The last temptation is the greatest treason:
> To do the right deed for the wrong reason.

Here Becket gives voice to the music of the beatitude, "Blessed are the pure of heart for they shall see God." The word *katharos* used in the Greek text for "pure" means unadulterated or unmixed. Unlike the cultic term *hagnos* used to describe physical purity and purifications required to draw near the holy, *katharos* addresses Jesus' concern for the inner posture of an act. It recalls other sayings like, "A good tree cannot bear bad fruit, or a poor tree good fruit" (Mt 7:18) and reflects the concern of all the beatitudes for the motive that underlies a person's behavior. When motive and act are one, the tree is like the one contemplated in W.B. Yeats' great poem, "Among School Children":

> O chestnut-tree, great-rooted blossomer,
> Are you the leaf, the blossom or the bole?
> O body swayed to music, O brightening glance,
> How can we tell the dancer from the dance?

In a less psychological age than ours, this beatitude may have been grasped more readily. The findings of modern psychology inform us that it is difficult to act from a clear and single motive, easy to fool ourselves about our often murky and complex intentions. An examination of conscience before the sacrament of reconciliation has among its goals clarification of the ambiguities clouding our motives. We know how hard such an examination is. Not so hard, however, is scrutinizing the behavior of others. It takes not much insight to see that they often act for other than their stated reasons.

Reflective persons scrutinize their own behavior as well as others', using the tools lying around contemporary households in the form of self-help books, Dear Abby columns, and memories of high school and college psychology courses. Because we think we know more about mixed motives than earlier generations, we are sometimes more tolerant of certain behaviors in ourselves and others. We try to use them to the good. Pastors do not discourage families from coming to church because the parents' intention is to "expose the children to religion." Pastors wish the parents knew their own need for God but trust that God can write straight with crooked lines.

A Presbyterian friend of mine invests her money in socially responsible businesses because John Calvin said one can do good while doing well. Philosophers of pragmatism teach mutuality as an ethical good because they think the best we can do by one another is maximize those areas of agreement where everybody gets something. Senior citizens, for example, should take college students as boarders because their presence in the house may provide protection against burglars or security in case of an accident.

Likewise, many persons join political coalitions that unite wildly diverse people who have in common just one point they are trying to make, or one goal they hope to achieve. In a nearby county feminist organizations and activists from the religious right have banded together to fight a mail order pornography business. The two groups agree on nothing but their belief that pornography hurts women. Their leaders state that they are merely taking a utilitarian approach. Similarly, negotiators of peace treaties do not ask the warring sides to give up their "wrong-headedness" on a host of issues in order to reach an accord; they require merely a laying aside of ideology in order to arrive at some necessary points of agreement. Unmixed motives are not a *sine qua non* for successful coalitions or treaties.

Most of us function as compromisers in family, church, and society. Becket worked this way for some time with the king who eventually martyred him, as did St. Thomas More with Henry VIII. It is a reasonable and effective way to proceed.

But compromise, even in the interest of progress or peace, is not purity of heart. The pastor who is pure of heart might feel compelled to tell parents that they should come to church to meet God themselves and not merely to introduce their children to God. The financial counsellor who is pure of heart might advise investors to forget about doing well and put their money instead into the most do-gooder, even if risky and extreme, enterprises, or better yet, to give their money away. In negotiations, purity of heart comes into play at a turning point or an impasse, when compromise can save the day but would infringe on one party's understanding of the good. In moments of crisis, Gandhi often frustrated his waiting colleagues while he prayed for clarity about the next step. The obvious compromise, in his view, did not necessarily favor the long range objective of freedom for India.

Purity of heart resides in the conscience of the individual who comes to realize, gradually or suddenly, like St. Paul knocked from his horse, that he or she has been on the wrong road. Paul's and Jesus' tradition, unlike our culture, stipulated purity of heart. Psalm 24:3 asks and answers:

Who may go up the mountain of the Lord?

And who may stand in his holy place?
[The one] who has clean hands and a pure heart.

And Proverbs 22:11 describes the choice between masters:

The Lord loves a sincere [person];
but you will make a king your friend with
   your fine phrases.

So, not surprisingly, Jesus condemns most severely not those who deny God and embrace only mammon, but the lukewarm who juggle loyalties to both masters. "If your right eye is your undoing, tear it out and fling it away; it is better for you to lose one part of your body than for the whole of it to be thrown into hell" (Mt 5:29). Temporizers need not apply.

Totally concentrated on the will of his Father, Jesus was pure in heart. His motives were unmixed. He wants ours to be the same. Kierkegaard says, "Purity of heart is to will one thing," but the exercise of will without the vision of Jesus leads to self-delusion and fanaticism. We rightly suspect an Elmer Gantry in every zealot. Jesus himself rebuked the zeal of the disciples who became indignant when a woman poured over his head a bottle of costly oil. The oil could have been sold and the money given to the poor, they cried, but Jesus answered: "You have the poor among you always; but you will not always have me" (Mt 28:11). The presence of Jesus constitutes the dividing line between zeal and purity of heart.

Many learn to dwell in the presence of God because they have discovered that there is nowhere else worth living. As Karl Jaspers says, "Once the idea of God penetrates the soul, there comes a fear of losing him and an unremitting impulse to do whatever might prevent God from disappearing."

The French mystic Simone Weil felt like this. Called the "Pilgrim of the Absolute" by one of her biographers, Weil defines prayer as "absolutely unmixed attention" (Weil, *Gravity and Grace*, p. 172). Unmixed, as in *katharos*. Elsewhere she says that "God is attention without distraction" (Weil,

Reader, p. 425). Her poem, "The Stars," describes this difficult posture and how it leads to the heart's purification. Through attention, we allow God to tear us from the mixed motives of the past and hurl us into tomorrow's purity of heart.

Fiery stars peopling the night the far skies,
Mute stars turning without seeing always icy,
You tear from our hearts the day past
And hurl us into tomorrow, our cries lost at your height.
Since we must, we follow you, with arms tied,
With eyes raised toward your pure but bitter light.
On your face all traces matter little.
We hold our tongues, we stagger on the highways.
It is there, in the heart suddenly, their fire divine
(Weil, *Reader*, p. 409).

Those who have tried to pray know how difficult unadulterated attention is. We feel our arms tied, our eyes raised, but our brains resound with a million thoughts. The most creative ideas seem to come, in fact, precisely when we try not to have ideas, but to pray. Many forms of meditation aim to teach us to limit the mind's interference. Zen, the Jesus Prayer, and "centering" are among them. Distracting thoughts may course through the brain, these methods admonish, but one simply returns the attention to the heart or to the breath, which carries life to both heart and brain. That way, attention can remain undivided. Because of distractions, one may rarely feel attentive, however. Those who have meditated for years stress the need for faith rather than measuring attention.

"With eyes raised toward your pure but bitter light," says Weil. "Blessed are the pure for they shall see," says Jesus, and he elsewhere emphasizes the importance of seeing. He explains to the disciples that he speaks in parables because of those who "look without seeing and listen without hearing or understanding," and he recalls the excoriating prophecy of Isaiah:

Their ears are deafened and their eyes blinded,

so that they cannot see with their eyes
nor listen with their ears
nor understand with their wits
so that they may turn and be healed (Is 6:10).

Jesus implies that the disciples differ from other Jews, especially the Pharisees, who look without seeing and listen without hearing. And for the disciples, those who do see, he offers the same macarismic form as the beatitudes, "Blessed are your eyes, for they see" (Mt 13:16, *RSV*). Because they are willing to see, to watch and look and listen hard enough to learn understanding, they can become pure of heart. Conversely, the pure of heart are blessed because they see God and the things of God.

So important is the eye that elsewhere Jesus judges it should be torn out if it offends. The eye relates to purity of heart insofar as it is an organ of perception, the means of vision. We see what we can, what the heart allows us to see. St. Paul says, "To the pure all things are pure" (Ti 1:15), and St. Thomas Aquinas holds that knowledge is perceived according to the mode of the knower. What we are able to perceive is a function of who we are.

My perception may limit me. For example, when I watch a Japanese *kabuki* play, I may admire the movement and costume. But because I have no feel for the characters' cultural significance, I remain ultimately unmoved. I do not really see the play. Someone who doesn't get a joke likewise has her mind on things other than the referents the joke depends on. One person's getting or failing to get a joke can affect the response of the whole group. We laugh harder when the world laughs with us. Perception, or the lack of it, can alter the humor, the pathos, the meaning of a situation. It is a vital part of the total context.

Psychiatrist Rollo May in his *Power and Innocence*, argues in fact that an "innocent" can alter reality by being pure of heart. May defines authentic innocence as the preservation of a childlike clarity in adulthood from which awe and wonder may come. It leads to spirituality, as in St. Francis' relationship with the birds and even the wolf, but does not sacrifice reality by denying evil, though it can be a protection from it. May recalls a woman who grew up in war-torn Germany telling of French and Moroccan troops who took their town and raped whatever girls they could find.

> Though thirteen years of age (and they were raping nine-year-olds), she could walk unmolested through a group of soldiers because she knew nothing about sexual intercourse or what men did. Her complete innocence, she believed, saved her; if she had had any kind of experience, the flicker of her eyelash or an unplanned glance, perhaps of fear, would have been enough enticement—as a dog bites the person whose fear it smells—for the rampaging soldiers to grab her also (May, p. 49).

In this situation the girl's purity of heart, what she saw and could not see, understood and did not understand, protected her because it affected in turn the perceptions of the soldiers around her.

If to the pure of heart all things are pure, we might ponder what they are to the impure, to those with "mixed" motives. If I am honest partly because it is good to be honest and partly because I don't like to get caught at being dishonest, I expect that others behave honestly for a similar mix of motives. I inevitably treat them differently than I would if I believed they were incorruptible because of their love of the good. I am more cautious, more watchful. This is common sense. The problem is, as someone has said, if we are on guard duty, we tend to see only thieves.

If we are not ourselves pure of heart, in other words, we may not be able to recognize when others are. When another nation offers a peace initiative—as the Soviet Union did when it unilaterally ceased some nuclear testing in the 1980s—the *only* question U.S. government leaders and media personalities asked was, "What will the Soviets get out of this proposal?" Such a skeptical stance makes it impossible to see the good where it arises.

If enough people lack purity of heart, they create a world where it cannot exist, where all people are always suspicious. Much of our world is like that now. Some make fortunes selling "security systems," others waging lawsuits for malpractice. U.S. embassies abroad are identifiable by their high walls, barbed wire, and the military personnel searching visitors at the gate. In many Latin American countries homes in wealthy neighborhoods top their fences with broken glass. Ten years ago I was startled to see an armed security guard posted at an ice cream store in a mini-mall in the capital of Honduras. Since then such guards have become common sights in the U.S., if not yet at ice cream stores, then certainly at banks and malls.

These physical manifestations of our suspicion of others are merely external symbols of a fear that often seems justified. A recently retired elementary school principal told me that she thinks our children have lost their childhood. We have left no room for spontaneity, she thinks, and without spontaneity both play and creativity vanish. Responsible parents feel they must schedule every minute of their children's lives and warn them against danger everywhere. Youngsters must be picked up at school, taken to supervised lessons or scout meetings, and escorted home to play within sight of their or someone else's parents.

The principal did not condemn parents who are careful, but lamented the fact that they need to be. She and I can remember a childhood when we wandered home after school by way of friends' houses or a local playground, and when whole summer days were spent frolicking at a public pool, or wandering the city or countryside with friends. Today, such carefree childhoods abide mainly in the realm of nostalgia.

If our lack of pure hearts keeps us from finding purity in others and freedom in the places we live, do we not then live in a kind of exile? Isaiah says, "My people will go into exile from want of perception" (Is 5:13, *JB*). And "without vision the people perish." We cannot long endure without vision, a clear and unadulterated perception of who we are or can be in relationship to others in the world, and above all in relationship to God. If we are not steadfastly fixed, like Jesus, on the will of the Father, we need to ask ourselves what other motives have entered into our reckonings. What or who is the mammon who vies with God for our hearts?

In muddled or roundabout ways many do ask this question. We have "mid-life crises," for example, or find other socially acceptable ways to check on who we are and where we are going. Sometimes at age forty, people who have hitherto been driven either to make a million or to change the world sit back and take account of what is driving them. I know one hard-bitten labor organizer who began to dance at the age of forty-five as an expression of his new found sense that he had to give up trying to control events. Our local paper recently carried an article about a thirty-eight-year-old former millionaire now working in a clothing store. He chose to go into bankruptcy in order to distance himself from the mammon of commodities trading in the eighties. He came to "see" himself and did not like what he saw.

Both of these men are moving toward purity of heart, though they might not put it that way. We all so move when we ask ourselves what the mix of our motives is and resolve to refine them in God's fire, to winnow them in the fan of God's love. We will then find ourselves better able to see.

"Blessed are the pure of heart, for they shall see God" has been called the mystic's beatitude. Its fruit is vision, one that has usually been "purified in a refining fire." In Jesus' tradition, only two mortals, Moses and Elijah, saw God and lived. Actually, they heard God's voice, as did the apostles at the transfiguration, but believers refer to the experience of God as seeing. Across the centuries saints and visionaries from all religions have seen God as they prayed or labored or sat under trees. Most have simplified or more intensely focused their lives after the experience. Indeed, their daily lives may actually have become more complicated for the new or added commitments their vision led them to, but as their motives became purer, less mixed, they more steadily walked a straight path through the complexity.

In his book, *And There Was Light*, Jacques Lusseyran describes this experience. A young blind man in France at the start of World War II, Lusseyran did not think he could affect the German occupation of his country. Then he got measles, and in the first few hours of fever, he felt his system pouring out foreign bodies, a poison as much moral as physical. He realized "the occupation is my sickness" and proceeded to organize fellow students into a nonviolent resistance movement that eventually distributed hundreds of thousands of alternative newspapers under the noses of the occupiers and their collaborators. Meanwhile, he also pursued intense university studies.

Each morning Lusseyran prayed before he went to his tasks, which included the admission of new members to the movement. All potential recruits had to meet with "the blind one" and pass the test of his "seeing" their worth. Additionally, his memory was the only database for the movement. It held more than a thousand Paris telephone numbers and a plethora of academic information about Leibniz, Turkish history, and the letters of Cicero. Each Sunday, to wipe away the mental strain, Lusseyran took a fifteen mile hike with a friend. "At night we were dead tired," he recounts. "The next day, when we got up at five o'clock, it was as if it were the first day of the world." He was pure of heart. He understood the liberation of France to be God's work, focused on it intensely, and consequently could see clearly people and the freshness of the world in the midst of chaos.

Great artists also offer a vision. Immediately we think of Michelangelo, Shakespeare, and Van Gogh. But contemporary, even popular artists, may also demonstrate vision. Paul Simon's *Graceland*, or the *Missa Gaia* of the Paul Winter consort, for example, show us things about our world that we might otherwise miss. The former fuses lyrics and music to point to grace in the midst of crisis and banality, if we but see. Despite the confusion and secularism of "the automatic earth," a "story of how we begin to remember" is possible, says Simon, through a return to the "roots of rhythm," real things that remain beyond the ephemeral.

In Winter's work, animal sounds establish rhythm and tone. Drums, flutes, and tenor saxophone reiterate the clicks of whales, squeals of seal pups, and howls of wolves. Human music becomes purer as it reflects the animals'. It becomes simpler, sometimes with melody only, as in plain chant. The music envisions and enacts harmony among the species. Both Simon and Winter have a vision of how human life might be. Their visions refract in miniature the incarnation of Jesus who also came to show us also what human life might be.

Some artists' visions become the means for others to achieve insight and be able to aim their lives more directly at God. It was architecture that first moved Simone Weil to pray. In a letter to her Dominican adviser, she wrote about her 1937 visit to Assisi: "There, alone in the little twelfth century Romanesque chapel, an incomparable marvel of purity where Saint Francis often used to pray, something stronger than I compelled me for the first time in my life to go down in my knees" (Weil, *Reader*, p. 15). The purity of the chapel spoke to the single-mindedness of her life up to that time. George Herbert's poem "Love," memorized by Weil about this same time in her life, also helped her to focus her attention with joy and tenderness.

At certain times vision may visit any of us; in such moments we experience ever so briefly the simplicity of life lived under the eye of God. Being in nature or in some other holy place, meditation, or the contemplation of a work of art may facilitate these moments. The following recalls such a fleeting vision of peace experienced on a boat in the Sea of Galilee a few years ago.

To meet with silence
set out in the boat
    early or late (time doesn't count)

Leave your cameras home and thermos jugs
it can't be recorded or provided for

If you take a friend
both must understand
that at such moments
you are always alone
and only your shadows
may overlap

Push off directly from the shore
    (to be tentative is to drift)
and plant your oars
like sunflower seeds
in undulant rows

When you arrive
somewhere in the middle of things
pull up the oars
    again with steady hand
and fix your gaze
    not on the shore
but on water or sky
or the slivers that circle
your empty craft

No birds will sing
nor waves clap

If the sun shines
a mist will veil it
and crinkle the skin
on the back of your neck

When it is done
you may paddle home
with original wings

Being in a beautiful or holy place may send us away renewed, simplified, more committed to purity of heart. But vision usually arises in a life lived in the attempt to unmix motives and hold fast to the will of God, often in trying circumstances. In El Salvador in 1989 I heard the sermon of the Lutheran Bishop Medardo Gomez whose young family had been targeted by death squads and whose church had been bombed. In his courage and peaceful manner, he reminded many Salvadorans of the martyred Roman Catholic Archbishop Oscar Romero. One humid Sunday morning, in his small church, windows open to the street a short distance from a military garrison, Medardo proclaimed in gentle tones a gospel vision for his people. Here is a rough translation of it:

> Brothers and Sisters! St. Luke's gospel for this second Sunday before Easter tells us how beautiful was the vineyard, the cosmos, at its first creation. In its origin it was well-ordered, and our country too was beautiful, a paradise where God had put enough for all.
>
> The owner of the vineyard, who is God, put some administrators in charge who disrupted the order of creation. They took it for themselves and killed, assassinated those who came from the owner to remind them of his wishes. They killed the prophets, including Jesus. They converted the paradise of the vineyard into an inferno.
>
> So the Lord of the vineyard decided to give it into the hands of other workers, to those of us who wish our country to return to being paradise, a land of milk and honey. We must pray that we have wisdom and strength to be better workers, better administrators than those who have gone before. It is quite possible too, and we have seen it in our daily lives, that the unjust administrators will kill those prophets among us who try to accomplish the will of the owner, of God, and we know that

those prophets and martyrs help to create the new space, the new creation that cannot fail to come to be.

Announcements now: three children were killed on Wednesday because of the placement of mines. We ask the F.M.L.N. and the government to refrain from violence. It kills mainly the innocent.

This next week is important because of the elections. We ordinary people are caught in the middle. The armed forces say to vote; the F.M.L.N. tells us not to vote. What are we to do?

On Thursday will be a demonstration for peace in the Plaza Civica de San Salvador. It has nothing to do with the parties; it has nothing to do with voting. It is a demonstration for peace. It is the people of God on their pilgrimage. I go as a bishop, as a pastor, to call the groups who come, the army, the popular organizations, not to use violence. We will be there lined up, as a church, among the thousands. We will bring our sons and daughters, our children, to demand there not be violence. We will not be afraid as we march in communion with God toward the land flowing with milk and honey. Away from the inferno where thousands are born condemned to death, their lives lived only for a few days.

We remember to pray for peace during this important week, that the armed forces and the parties support the proposal for peace, that outside forces like the United States, the government that commands in a subtle way, use its power toward negotiations.

We pray too that the many who have left our country out of fear, have left our paradise to go north, may return to paradise, return to find the land of milk and honey here, return to find we have no inferno anymore.

My people, let us pray!

Thomas Merton, a model for many contemporary seekers, apparently was blessed with a vision also when he visited a Buddhist shrine in Sri Lanka during his trip to the East before he died:

> Looking at these figures [of the Buddha] I was suddenly, almost forcibly jerked clean out of the habitual, half-tied vision of things, and an inner clearness, clarity, as if exploding from the rocks themselves became evident and obvious. ... All problems are resolved and everything is clear. The rocks, all matter, all life, is charged with *dharmakaya* ... everything is emptiness and everything is compassion. I don't know when in my life I have ever had such a sense of beauty and spiritual validity running together (Merton, pp. 233-234).

Merton's autobiography, and many of his journals and letters, show the struggles of a person not without flaws but persistent in the search for his true self, the self that is simple and pure of heart, whose motives are unmixed and uncompromising. His friends are happy that this man of pure heart had the consolation of seeing God before he died. It gives hope to all who struggle to live as he and Jesus did, wanting only to do God's will in this world. We trust that we are blessed by the presence of God even as we struggle. On occasion, we can even see that blessing.

7

Blessed Are the Peacemakers

Most tribal religions have gods of war, fewer have goddesses of peace. Eirene, the Greeks' divine personification of peace, had little mythology or cult. But a famous statue shows her holding the infant Wealth, and a song by Bacchylides extols wealth, music, and dance as Eirene's gifts. *Eirene* is the word for peace in the Greek translation of "Blessed are the peacemakers for they shall be called children of God." It connotes "absence of trouble" whereas the Hebrew *shalom* denotes "fullness of good." *Shalom* and its Arabic cognate *salaam* remain standard greetings in half the world. The greeter hopes the one greeted will know abundance, fullness of life, and right relationships.

The Jewish rabbis stressed right relationships as the basis for peace. As Pope Paul VI said, "If you want peace, work for justice." Their emphases recall that the beatitude invites us to peacemaking or peacedoing, not merely to peaceloving. It rejects passivity, though it may bless pacifists. Jesus went about not merely loving good, but also doing good. If no one makes the effort to right relationships, they will not be right. They do not spring whole and entire out of the head of the dreamer. God is ultimately the peacemaker and indeed is peace itself, but to be like God we must make peace in God's name. We have to take the initiative to untangle the knots in the personal and communal webs we inhabit.

Peacemaking is not for the passive. The great apostle of nonviolence, Mahatma Gandhi, thought initiative so crucial that he ranked inaction in the face of evil last, after both nonviolent action and violent action. He thought it better to be a sincere soldier than a wobbling pacifist, urging the Pathans people of northwest India to continue using physical force until they were convinced that nonviolent action was right. His admonition recalls the Quaker founder George Fox counselling his follower William Penn, who was having qualms about carrying a sword as an emblem of rank, "Wear it as long as thou canst."

Like their forebears, many modern Quakers have honed their skills in actively righting relationships. One day I stopped by to see an elderly Roman Catholic monsignor I knew. As I entered the room he hung up the phone, ruefully nodding his head. He had just been called by a local Quaker who read in the paper that some Native American neighbors had lost their cultural center in a fire. The Friend was canvassing the local clergy to see how they could help replace the center. "You know," said Monsignor, his Irish brogue dancing along the words, "I read that same article in the paper and said to myself, What a shame. The Quakers read it and took action. What's the difference between us?"

The difference lies in taking the first step. Like Jesus, the great practitioners of nonviolence have been doers of the word, makers of peace, not merely those who admire or applaud or hope for it. Gandhi called his mission *satyagraha*, truth force, a concept more lively than the traditional *ahimsa*, the renunciation of the will or desire to kill or do harm. He moved beyond Hindu tradition to study Jesus and western proponents of nonviolence like Thoreau and Tolstoy. In *Nonviolence in Peace and War*, Gandhi writes that his notion of nonviolence is active, a "more real fighting against wickedness than retaliation whose very nature is to increase wickedness" (in Ferguson, p. 38).

Instead of throwing more wood on the fire of violence, Gandhi would quench it with the water of spiritual resistance. Or, to use his own metaphor,

> I seek entirely to blunt the edge of the tyrant's sword not by putting up against it a sharper-edged weapon, but by disappointing his expectation that I would be offering physical resistance. The resistance of the soul that I should offer instead would elude him. It would at first dazzle him, and at last compel recognition from him, which recognition would not humiliate him but would uplift him" (in Ferguson, p. 38).

Employing his "resistance of the soul," Gandhi freed India of British domination. Using similar weapons, Martin Luther King struggled for civil rights for African-Americans in the United States. Dorothy Day established houses of hospitality, published *The Catholic Worker*, and led the New York City protest against preparations for nuclear war in the 1950s. Danilo Dolci fought the mafia in Sicily. Caesar Chavez organized "unorganizeable" farmworkers. Archbishop Desmond Tutu awakened churches in South Africa and throughout the world to the blasphemy of apartheid. Archbishop Oscar Romero stood against the violence of both government and revolutionaries in El Salvador. Apostles of nonviolent action, they all loved peace but, more importantly, they made it. They were doers of the word.

Peacemaking makes demands even as it blesses. It will not be invoked to smooth over skewed relationships or to defend injustice. If I know my son is using drugs but I don't confront him for fear he will run away from home, I am not a peacemaker. If I suspect my neighbor of child abuse and fail to call the appropriate authorities, I am not a peacemaker. If I live in a mining town where people carry jugs of water for drinking and bathing as they pass the mine owner's swimming pool and I do nothing, I am not a peacemaker.

I may be called "idealistic" or a "disturber of the peace" for questioning wrong relationships, but my doing so acknowledges the deeper reality that will not forever be denied. This questioning Archbishop Romero did in a homily for the feast of the Epiphany:

> Do not consider me, please, as an enemy. I am simply a shepherd, a brother, a friend of this people—one who knows their suffering, their hungers, their anguish. It is in the name of these voices that I raise my voice to say: Do not idolize your wealth! Do not hoard it and let the rest die of hunger! Share! So that you may be happy. … We must know how to strip ourselves of our rings so that they won't be cut off our fingers. I think it's a very illustrative expression. Whoever isn't willing to do without his rings risks having them cut off his hand. Whoever isn't willing to give out of love and social justice makes mandatory that his luxuries be taken away by violence.

Romero does not judge so much as acknowledge those relationships that sooner or later will be righted. He echoes the writer of the most practical epistle, the letter of James, who also traces violence to the defense of wrong relationships:

> What causes conflicts and quarrels among you? Do they not spring from the aggressiveness of your bodily desires? You want something which you cannot have, and so you are bent on murder (Jas 4:1-2).

Failure to confront wrong relationships because of attachment to a false peace is the opposite of peacemaking or nonviolence. So is passive aggression, a refusal to put one's cards on the table we sit at with other human beings. I have lived in community with sisters who submerged in silence their objections to house policy or their differences with other community members. They may have believed they were holy because they did not complain, but their silence spoke eloquently their disapproval or dissatisfaction, as did their behavior.

One time I observed the "meekest" of sisters mercilessly tongue-lash the work supervisor of an ex-prisoner who lived with the sister in a halfway house. Told by the young woman that her supervisor had underpaid her on the job, the sister failed to ask any questions of the supervisor before lacerating him with accusations. Stunned by her assumption that he was guilty and by her excoriating tone, I had to conclude that it overflowed from her own pent-up inability to confront those she felt had wronged her. Her aggression had little to do with the supervisor and ex-prisoner. Nor did it right any relationships. My usually mild-mannered companion was not a peacemaker.

The peacemaker risks vulnerability. The disciples went forth without staff or sandals. Those who ask governments to lay down their weapons had better be willing to live a disarmed life themselves. Most of us would rather risk our lives than feel like a fool, but peacemaking may require both. I hesitate to risk the small pains of laughter and rebuff, to stand in a silent vigil on a public street where sensible people might walk by and think I'm crazy, to get my picture in the paper holding a sign that may make me the dinner conversation of my more sophisticated acquaintances, to make the first overture in a fractured relationship when I have reason to believe the response will be rejection or a sneer.

Fear of failure runs even deeper than the risk of looking ridiculous. In his 1986 book-length interview *Disturbing the Peace*, Václav Havel responds to a Czech exile's criticism that petitions don't offer much hope for changing governments. People who evaluate things too objectively, "from above," says Havel, want to see immediate results. "They don't have a lot of sympathy for acts which can only be evaluated years after they take place, which are motivated by moral factors, and which therefore run the risk of never accomplishing anything." Fear of this risk can keep people from perceiving the "mysterious ambiguity of human behavior" and can thus prevent peace.

When Luther nailed his theses to the Wittenberg Cathedral door, when Dr. King undertook the Montgomery bus boycott, when millions of people marched to protest the Vietnam War: for all they knew, the world would little note nor long remember what they did. Peacemakers toss moral pennies in remote fountains, set paper boats to sail on dangerous rapids, dare to unwrap for the world's scorn those foolish treasures they carry next to their hearts.

Peacemakers must be imaginative as well as vulnerable. Those who contribute to violence, wrong relationships, or who merely observe it passively, behave so partly from lack of imagination. They cannot intuit how the victim feels, perhaps. Or they accept that there is nothing new under the sun, where "the poor you have always with you." Or they are schooled to respond to evil automatically by hitting back with more. They are, as Robert Frost says, unable to go beyond their father's saying, to think of or seek out creative responses.

Responding in kind to violence creates new sources of violence in the world, however. The evil spirals farther out and up and around. What we deplore in our enemy now has a livelier hold on us than before and, as some have noted, we become like the enemy, at times a mirror image. On my personal battlefield with a spiteful spouse or a sullen teen, I may use weapons of words or silence because I am at a loss for imagining how to de-escalate the conflict. I don't want to raise the white flag and I don't know how to bound across the pockmarked landscape with a wholehearted embrace. On a grander scale, nations do the same, pitching across borders harsher and harsher accusations until the first air bombardment in the middle of the night seems almost a relief to the world looking on and longing for a climax.

Simone Weil deplored the means used by the allies to defeat Hitler in World War II because she saw that the future would be transformed by the magnitude of the trust in violence that effort entailed. In her provocative essay on "*The Iliad* as a Poem of Force," she examines Homer's characterizations of great men who as they fight on become more and more automatic in their actions, more like beasts or machines, in order to endure the relentless onslaughts of battle. Many would say Weil's vision of the post-war future has come to be.

The poet responds, "Imagine the world." Imagine what else could be happening at this moment. Imagine how Jesus or Buddha or Gandhi would act. Imagine beyond the narrow horizon of hurt and the moment's cry for reacting in kind. Mary did this in her Magnificat. She dared to imagine the world turned upside down by the coming of her child, who would render a servant woman great. Yahweh pulls down the mighty from their thrones and exalts the lowly, she proclaims, fills the hungry and sends the rich away empty. Not in the world she saw around her, certainly, where people like her became refugees in the dark of night because of some petty potentate's paranoia.

Her son's imagination at least equalled Mary's. His use of parables, allegory and metaphor, told his truth "aslant," as Emily Dickinson would say, so it would be clearer to the poor and simple, infuriatingly noncommittal for the rational and judgmental. When asked to be a judge himself, he turned the question back on the questioners. Arbitration of a quarrel between two brothers: "Who made me judge over you?" Deciding the fate of a woman caught in adultery: "Let him who is without sin throw the first stone." Determining the relevance of the Law in his new dispensation:

> You have learned that they were told, "Eye for eye, tooth for tooth." But what I tell you is this: Do not set yourself against the man who wrongs you. If someone slaps you on the right cheek, turn and offer him your left. If a man wants to sue you for your shirt, let him have your coat as well. If a man in authority makes you go one mile, go with him two (Mt 5:38-41).

Jesus does not deny enemies are real. They will hurt and humiliate us. But we are charged with being alert, taking them off guard, upending their enslaving plans for us. Remind them that we are human too, throw in their faces the cold water of our power to choose—or not to choose—a method of collaboration.

Some thinkers believe that the causes of war lie in imaginations that tolerate the thought of violence. Others hold that war arises from minds unable to birth images of alternatives to it. What if we simply said no to it? Refused to harbor the image of violence? Could our minds allow the vacuum? Would they throw up alternative, nonviolent images? In his mammoth work, *The Politics of Nonviolent Action*, Gene Sharpe spells out fifty-four nonviolent strategies for resolving conflict—boycotts, fasting, strikes, demonstrations, petitions, sit-ins, defiance of blockades, noncooperation with conscription. Applied with timeliness, each has at least as much chance of righting relationships as violence does.

The means are there for those with heart and hands and head creative enough to pluck them from the air. What does a butterfly do in the path of a bulldozer? The response rests with imagination and the patience and hope that enable it.

In 1983, when the Reagan-contra war against the Nicaraguan people had already claimed thousands of lives, thirty people from almost as many North Carolina churches traveled to Nicaragua after Easter to see for ourselves what was happening. One day we clattered along on a bus toward the Honduran border, crossing on rickety bridges over minuscule Rio Grandes and fording streams where the bridges had been washed out or blown up. We arrived at Jalapa, a rural farming town, just as the community was mourning the destruction of its cooperative barns and the wounding of two children who later died. Jalapa sat within sight of the Honduran border, and in the sites of contra guns on the hills. We spent the day there, listening to and praying with the mourners, but we decided to leave in time to avoid being on the road after dark.

The next day we heard that Jalapa had been bombed again, after we left. Angered by this close-up look at what our tax money was buying, we also felt guilty that we had not stayed overnight in Jalapa. As we discussed the event and its implications, one of the travellers joked: "Since they bombed *before* and *after* but not *while* we were there, maybe we need to keep North Americans in Jalapa all the time." We laughed at the joke but kept circling back to it in conversation. We knew that as visitors to Jalapa we were visible to the contras on the border, who would wish to avoid the embarrassment of killing U.S. citizens.

For the next few days we thought seriously about what had been said in jest, and when we returned to Managua and the U.S., we put before some political thinkers and organizers the question, "What if we could keep enough Americans at the border to make it politically awkward for the contras to shoot?" Thus, born in a joke was Witness for Peace, an organization that eventually placed four thousand long and short term volunteers in Nicaragua over a period of eight years, volunteers who lived with the people, documented contra atrocities for the U.S. media, and—in the opinion of many Nicaraguans—helped prevent a direct U.S. invasion of that country.

Moreover, Witness for Peace awakened many of the North American volunteers to a new way of thinking. They were challenged to take risks and to imagine alternative relationships between Nicaraguan and North American people. Like many nonviolent efforts, Witness for Peace utilized some inventive strategies along the way: documenting stories, helping to harvest coffee and beans, renting a shrimp boat to head off a U.S. navy destroyer, launching a Peace Flotilla on the River San Juan, planting crosses across America that bore the names of the Nicaraguan dead, holding prayer services in churches and parks. These were actions for their time not unlike Gandhi's salt march, the altering of Czech train signs in World War II, and Martin Luther King's sending children to face the fire hoses.

If peacemaking requires initiative, vulnerability, and imagination, what is its opposite? It is the same old world gone wrong and accepted as a given. It is to recite "the poor you have always with you" as an alternative to offering a hand. It is the language of "realistic" solutions, ultimatums, advertising, and other lies. And we live in such haste, itself a form of violence, that we fail to examine the language.

Only something transcendent to the human spirit motivates the peacemaker. We do not normally pause to examine how violence works. We do not naturally abhor it, rooted as it is in our own ego and greed. Journalists rush to cover wars. Americans love action movies where action means lots of weapons and blood. We all cheer when the bully gets trounced by the ninety-nine pound weakling. We like violence when we are not its victim. We applaud until it turns on us. But our insight fails us when we don't realize that, unchecked, it will inevitably turn to grip us by the throat.

We speak a language of ultimatum rather than negotiation. Nonviolent initiatives must be timely. With delay, conflicts fester, and showdown seems the only recourse. Our children grow undisciplined over months or years of inattention to their manners or tantrums or deceptions, and suddenly we draw the line. Then our means are drastic. We have to beat them or order them out of our houses and lives. As a nation, we enable dictators like Manuel Noriega, Saddam Hussein, and Anastasio Somoza and then decide, when their behavior no longer suits us, that they must be bombed, kidnapped, or otherwise disposed of.

Perhaps, because women are more likely victims of violence, they have had to learn to rely on negotiation more than ultimatums. Perhaps women—consigned most of the care for children, the old, and the sick—have simply had to develop more patience—and creativity. A friend who grew up with ten brothers and sisters says she marvels at her mother's gift for diverting. Her mother would look into the back yard from the kitchen window, see one child hitting, tweaking, or pummeling another, and deftly remark, "It's time to bake cookies," or "Look at that monarch butterfly by the sandpile," or "Do you want peanut butter or tomato sandwiches for lunch?" Baited thus, both victim and victimizer quickly refocused their attention.

Women have a long history of trying to hold families together despite their routine centripetal spinning. Women generally make better peacemakers than men because, as the chief nurturers, they sense that the family can't go on without a measure of peace and know that the family must go on. Peacemakers, like feminists, should work to put a man in every nursery for every woman who enters the work force. Let each sex learn the other's traditional skills.

We can dispute whether the cause is cultural or genetic, but studies show that little girls are more likely than little boys to draw everyone into the play group, less likely to force showdowns or make rules to keep some out. For whatever reason, women's language tends to be more open-ended and receptive to dialogue than men's. Some will be quick to remind me of Golda Meir and Margaret Thatcher, hardly models for peacemaking. But I prefer to think of the hundreds of women I know who have not developed so-called "male coping skills," who would understand the comments of Palestinian peace negotiator Hanan Ashrawi, interviewed on National Public Radio not long ago. When asked whether the peace talks with Israel were likely to go anywhere, she replied, "They have to. Violence and military solutions do not work; they only lead to further problems." Most women I know believe that and try to act on it; most men I know tell their sons not to pick a fight, but not to "back down" from one either.

Because most corporate and political structures are controlled by men who won't "back down," we don't see much reliance on timely negotiation. Given the many outside pressures on women today, there may be less time for negotiation in the home as well. But where it happens, it holds us together, keeps our world from spinning apart.

We speak the language of violence. I heard the Russian poet Yevgeny Yevtushenko address this issue shortly after the breakup of the Soviet Union. An American in the audience asked him if there would be less censorship of pornography in Russia now. Yevtushenko responded, "The problem is not pornography, but war-nography." Actually, the problem is both, and the two are related. Both make objects out of persons and cloak that objectification in images or words. Yet, as Yevtushenko implied, war is killing us at every level of our being. Our defense of war, the indefensible, makes lies of our words, as when we speak of the civilian victims of U.S. Tomahawk missiles over Baghdad as "collateral damage."

In his 1946 essay "Politics and the English Language," George Orwell made the classic connection between language and behavior. Dead metaphors, pretentious diction, and meaningless words shield us from the bald horror of what we do. Not only is language debased, says Orwell, but its blurring of atrocities permits us to continue and even intensify them. The enlisted men who fire bombed retreating Iraqi soldiers as they tried to escape across the desert in the Persian Gulf War at least were graphic in naming what they did a "turkey shoot." Nevertheless, their language objectifies and distances almost as much as the Pentagon's language does.

The language of other bureaucracies—social services, education, health care, business, even religion—also distances. The pope and bishops demand "stringent moral criteria" for meeting "the requirements for a just war." But continuing to hold out the possibility of a just war in an age of nuclear weapons and other ingenuities of terrorism is an impious fiction. Children die. That is the definition of modern war. Innocents go unhoused and unhouseled to their graves—if they get graves. Just as church leaders cannot return us to the Middle Ages where the population clustered in the sheltering shadow of a monastery, they cannot will us back to rules in warfare that mandated fighting only between combatants who had time off for holy days. Pretending that such rules remain possible is to concur in the violence.

Religious leaders need a language of peace, one that condemns all wars, all violence, in concrete terms. It needs accompaniment by actions as concrete as Jesus' when he rebuked his disciple who cut off the ear of the man who came to arrest the master. Jesus picked up the ear and restored it to the man's face. When church leaders learn this language, they may be heeded. Why, despite warnings from Rome and some American bishops against the war with Iraq, were most prayers from pulpit and pew for the safety of U.S. soldiers? Catholics, like most Americans, did not seem to worry whether their nation was engaged in a just war and did not pray publicly for the children being bombed in Baghdad.

What if some bishops or the pope had gone to Baghdad and made their anti-war appeals from there? Would not that action have enabled both them and the bombers to think and speak more concretely about the consequences of the bombing? Who would call a dead bishop from the West "collateral damage"? The language of peacemaking is not the language of onlookers; it is the language of participants.

Imaginative language today is reserved mostly to unread poets and the advertising industry. Those who sell products know how, with clever words and images, to turn us into passive consumers of goods instead of active participants in the good. Unfortunately, our consumerism casts us in the role of Dives in Jesus' parable of the rich man and Lazarus. A child born in the United States today will use up thirty times more resources than a child born in Iraq. In the present world order, Iraqi and other third world children are fated to beg outside the gates of American and European children. The language of advertising conspires with the language of war to distract us from this fact. Peacemakers must break open this conspiracy of wrong relationships and deliver all our children from this fate.

Those who do so will be called children of God. Actually, they will be called "sons of God," "sons" from the Greek *huioi* or the Hebrew meaning "doing a god-like work." In *The Beatitudes in Context* Dennis Hamm notes that reaching for the inclusive "children of God" may make us miss the connection with other references to son(s) of God. The title "Son of God" often refers to Jesus. The beatitude promises "that peacemakers somehow participate in Jesus' obedient sonship" and share in the inclusive love described elsewhere in the Sermon on the Mount:

> You have learned that they were told, "Love your neighbor, hate your enemy." But what I tell you is this: Love your enemies and pray for your persecutors; only so can you be children of your heavenly Father, who makes his sun rise on good and bad alike, and sends the rain on the honest and the dishonest. If you love only those who love you, what reward can you expect? Surely the tax-gatherers do as much as that. And if you greet only your brothers, what is there extraordinary about that? Even the heathen do as much. There must be no limit to your goodness, as your heavenly Father's goodness knows no bounds (Mt 5:43-48).

Elsewhere Matthew also depicts Jesus as the antithesis of a warrior. Matthew 12:15-21 echoes a refrain from Isaiah 42:1-4 describing the mission of the *pais* (meaning either servant or son) who "will not break a bruised reed or snuff out a smoldering wick," and the triumphal entry into Jerusalem highlights the peaceful reign of the king who comes riding on a donkey. As Hamm indicates, both descriptions contrast with the warlike kingship of Jesus' ancestor David who ordered that the blind and lame be slain when he captured the capital. The peacemaker "sons of God" are more like the gentle Son of God who turns upside down the mission of the warrior king.

Peacemakers are blessed with the power of God, not the power of warriors and kings. To them, the world is gift not plunder, and their basic posture is gratitude for life as it comes from God. They believe that God's world still shines beneath the sear and smear of trade and toil. A friend of mine lived for twenty years among the native peoples of New Guinea whose culture valued neither competition nor violence. He describes the children as blooming with self-confidence and self-esteem. Like poor children everywhere, they had few clothes or toys, but everyone in the village loved and looked after them. The children lived out the first fruits of peace, he says. They knew who they were.

We would all like to know who we are, be the "sons of God" we are called to be, doing the work of God. The blessing is that we can. I met Dorothy Day a few years before her death, when she seemed at times less than fully present to what went on around her. But she knew who she was and she radiated peace. When Archbishop Desmond Tutu speaks, he can hardly keep his rich voice from laughter. He tells of his gratitude for prayers from around the world. "I met a hermit from Cal-i-forn-ia," he said one time, "who prays for me at 3 A.M. In Cal-i-forn-ia!" He repeated the name of the state, shaking his head and laughing at some wonderful, secret irony.

The Dalai Lama also laughs heartily, not despite the fact that his people are victims of genocide by the Chinese but because he holds the Chinese each day in his prayer of exchange. He prays to receive their anger and frustration and return to them the compassion he steadfastly practices. As he travels the world begging to be heard, he carries to his hearers a message and a laugh erupting from the same deep place as the rumbling prayers of Tibetan Buddhist monks.

In Jewish tradition, an image for peace is a man sitting under his own fig tree. The fig tree provides both shade and food, but needs many years to grow to maturity. Like peacemaking, a fig tree does not yield its abundance overnight. Doing this God-like work will not right all relationships the first time I take an initiative or a risk. But it does enable me to live more consciously as a "son of God."

Danilo Dolci, who gave up a future as an architect in Italy to help impoverished Sicilians build their own communities and took on the mafia in the process, lives his life with the intense, open heart that active nonviolence brings. He has risked much to serve as a bridge between individuals and to right relationships among groups. One of his biographers, Irving Howe, judges that Dolci represents "the possibility of an active goodness open to anyone, a 'saintliness' for which one need be no more than a man." Perhaps such a man is nothing less than a "son of God." Surely there is no greater blessing.

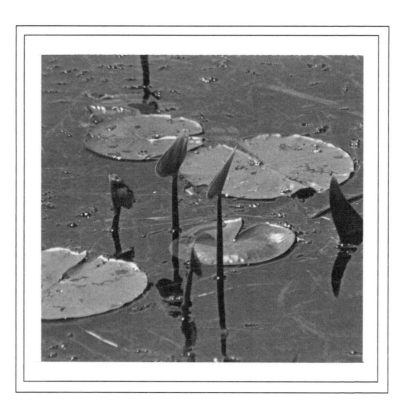

8

Blessed Are They Who Suffer Persecution for Justice Sake

Discipleship is disruption. The one who follows Jesus will have thoughts, feelings, relationships, work, and life itself stomped on, broken into, burglarized, ridiculed, and tossed aside. Life will seem a sieve the waters of time run through, leaving nothing behind but pebbles and broken pieces. Where was the true self I expected to find when I dedicated myself to finding God? Where the clarity and focus, identity and wholeness? Lost, it may seem, in the interruptions, revilings, and crucifixions that constitute the lot of the disciple.

The last beatitude recalls the fourth and rounds off the first. Those who hunger and thirst for justice will most likely be persecuted for it as well. Those who are persecuted become poor, even poorer than they were to begin with; but like the poor in spirit, they are gifted with the kingdom of heaven. Matthew uses the perfect participle in the passive voice, *dediogmenoi*, "those who have been persecuted," to remind the listeners that they already know what persecution is. They have tried to proselytize among the Jews and been slapped down for that. The verb tenses and moods in the following two, closely related verses indicate future persecu-

They have tried to proselytize among the Jews and been slapped down for that. The verb tenses and moods in the following two, closely related verses indicate future persecution as well. Hamm thinks those persecuted at any time because of their relationship to Jesus are blessed. Jesus himself connects that persecution with the treatment of prophets and indicates that wherever in the world justice is pursued, the persecution sure to follow blesses all seekers after justice.

Persecution wears more or less severe guises. It may be death; it may be disruption in the form of mere interruption. I once complained to a friend that frequent interruptions kept me from getting my work done. My friend responded, "Interruption is your work; it is the nature of ministry." I saw then that disruptions happened precisely because I claimed to do the work of a Christian. I did not choose to be with people whose lives were neat and orderly as the corners on a hospital bed; I chose to live and work with those for whom illness, loss, and minute eruptions of joy were the stuff of their days.

Daily disruptions are like water on a stone, a mild form of "persecution" wearing down patience. Vocational disruptions, however, can hurl the stone into a deep-flowing river. How many have, like Paul, been thrown from the sturdy horse they rode to a clear destination and told they were now to walk in bare feet on hot sand toward some always receding oasis that in their weaker moments they suspect is a mirage? How many have taken refuge in the belly of a friendly whale and found that it regurgitated them upon the very spot they fled from?

A prophetic man I knew, H. Shelton Smith, told me that when he had finished at Yale in the 1930s and was embarked on a challenging career teaching religion at Columbia University, he overheard a colleague comment that Smith would never return to his native South. There wouldn't be enough professional challenge there, said the colleague. The overheard comment provoked Smith to ask why the South could not keep its seed corn and led to his return to North

Carolina, where he subsequently founded the Duke University School of Religion and the North Carolina Council of Churches, and gave leadership to the civil rights movement in that state. Smith came to realize that his colleague's comment had been the voice of God disrupting his life.

Events other than voices can disrupt our lives. In his last talk before he died in the Far East, Thomas Merton spoke of the monk who had to flee Tibet when the Chinese invaded. The monk's last words to his fellow monks were, "From now on, brothers, everyone has to stand on his own two feet." In the name of discipleship, conscientious objectors, draft resisters, and religious reformers often find themselves standing alone or walking where they had not planned to go. The model for them all is Jesus, who came to understand more deeply as he lived it, the explosive nature of his mission to "speak truth to power."

Prophets are bound to be persecuted because they disrupt society, sometimes even before it disrupts their lives. Dietrich Bonhoeffer phrases this succinctly in *The Cost of Discipleship*: "When Christ calls a man he bids him come and die." How silly would be Christianity without the cross. It strikes us when we recall the anecdote about Clovis, King of the Franks, who heard the story of the crucifixion and vigorously asserted, "If I and my Frankish soldiers had been there, it would never have happened."

The persecution promised by Jesus manifests itself in myriad ways. In his commentary on Matthew, William Barclay notes those disruptions that arise from the need to earn a living. If an early Christian were a stonemason and his firm received a contract to build a temple to a heathen god, what was the disciple to do? One such man asked Tertullian, "What can I do? I must live!" Tertullian responded, "Must you?" Who of us has the courage to say to ourselves or to someone else whose work involves building weapons, depleting resources, marketing junk, propping up sick institutions, or selling health care or education as commodities, "Must you?" And yet, "the hand of the dyer is subdued by the dye in which it works." For Buddhists, the concept of "right occupation" is one-eighth of the Eightfold Noble Path proclaimed by Buddha as the way to enlightenment. "Right occupation," taken to heart, is bound to disrupt many lives in a society like ours that values material things over those of the spirit.

Persecution can also mean shunning by the church or some members of it. Matthew knew that his listeners had already suffered persecution prompted by Pharisees opposed to the teachings of Jesus. Jesus himself was killed by the Romans in collaboration with Jewish religious leaders. Until today, religious people persecute those who would call them to deeper faithfulness or new formulations of the truth. Attempts to coerce and suppress forward looking theologians are well known. After Vatican II many priests, sisters, bishops, and lay persons who tried to implement its insights in liturgy or religious education or social justice were excluded from participation in some church groups and labelled "modernist," "worldly," or "communist." Fully twenty years after the Council, a sister in contemporary dress could meet Roman Catholics who might ask, "Why don't you look like a real nun?" Some seemed genuinely unaware that their exclusionary language echoed that of the Pharisees.

I know a Methodist minister who was reassigned every year for twenty years because of his interracial efforts at whatever church he served. Another, a gifted pastor and preacher, lost his pastorate at one church and was refused others because he publicly favored human rights for gay and lesbian people. Several other ministers I know lost their churches when they signed a statement supporting the right of textile workers to organize. All of their churches thought of themselves as Christian.

For a member of the community of believers, the most hurtful persecution comes from the church, but the most dangerous may be meted out by the state that cannot bear the witness of truth. Archbishop Oscar Romero and Dietrich Bonhoeffer died when they confronted such states. Cardinal

Mindszenty was imprisoned by one for decades. Daniel and Philip Berrigan, Elizabeth McAllister, and other Plowshares activists have, among them, served hundreds of years in U.S. prisons because of their peace witness. Dom Helder Camara, the retired Brazilian archbishop, feared to leave his country because the government exploited his absence by arresting his pastoral workers and torturing them. They were more vulnerable than the well known archbishop, who was doubly pained that others had to suffer in his stead.

Some prophets do not necessarily claim to be Christian but do the work of Jesus by describing the possibility of a just order or by telling the truth about the terrible present. Alexander Solzhenitsyn earned prison and exile for this. Andrei Sakharov, Nelson Mandela, and Vaclav Havel spent time in jail or under house arrest. Steve Biko and Chris Hani were murdered in South Africa. Rigoberta Menchu had to flee Guatemala. For raising questions about "the disappeared," Argentinian newspaper editor Jacobo Timmerman was incarcerated, tortured and forced to emigrate to Israel. There he again took a prophetic stance, this time against Israel's war on Lebanon. For each of these famous persons, hundreds of thousands of unknown others have suffered similar fates.

Most of us avoid persecution, even in its mildest forms. Few desire martyrdom or even mild disruption of our lives. Our unwillingness to suffer often wears the mask of conformity to the status quo, which may be merely banal or utterly unspeakable. "Take care of number one, or who else will?" says the culture. If I do not put my family first, protecting them from the cruel world, what kind of person am I? One can imagine the rich man Dives offering excuses to Father Abraham for his failure to feed Lazarus begging at the gate. "But there were so many beggars. I would have been swallowed up by them. And my son was hanging out with the wrong crowd, my daughter having adolescent problems with self-esteem. They were my primary responsibility."

Just as individuals conform to the culture in order to avoid disruption, so do institutions, religious institutions among them. One thinks of the ecclesiastical allegiance to monarchy and other powers-that-were at the time of the French Revolution, the Russian Revolution, and the Mexican Revolution, and wonders how life might have been for the little people of these nations if the churches had taken their side. What if the Catholic and Protestant churches had not divided up pre-Mao China and proselytized the rice Christians while the masses starved around them? What if most Cuban church leaders had remained in Cuba and tried to work with Castro's government as some Christians did? What if the Vatican had not supported Haitian dictators even up to the time when, alone among governments, it granted diplomatic recognition to the military that ousted the elected President Aristide? One risk of conformity to the old, unjust order is losing the right to critique the new order as it comes into being.

In her book *The Re-Weaving of Religious Life,* Mary Jo Leddy faults North American religious communities today for their captivity to liberal capitalism and, by extension, she illuminates the cultural materialism of many religious people. She refers to Salvadoran theologian Jon Sobrino's reflections on personalist or liberal theologies that make religious life more "normal" than it was meant to be. Crises arise when those who have taken vows, instruments for radical commitment, no longer live life "in the desert or on the frontier" but attempt to have normal lifestyles and do normal work.

Sobrino asserts:

> If the apostolate and lifestyle have even a spark of madness about them, the vows will be an expression of the Christian folly of the cross. If, however, the apostolate and lifestyle are characterized by tidiness, adaptation, and acceptance of the comfortable center, then the vows will be seen, at least by the more perceptive, as responsible for a deep

division in the Christian and psychological consciousness of religion (in Leddy, p. 76).

What Sobrino and Leddy say about religious life applies
to Christians generally for, after all, what vow could be more
radical than faith in a crucified Jesus? In a feel-good culture
that prizes appearance and things, who would be more
marginal or eccentric than a Christian?

One consequence of the conformity of Christians wanting to avoid persecution is the pervading experience of the
"dark night" in our century. If more Christians were willing
to undergo the "dark night" of persecution, akin to the
mystical "dark night" described by St. John of the Cross,
perhaps fewer people in the world would be consigned to
the "dark night" of meaninglessness. Call it the absurd, the
death of meaning, or the end of God, but the failure of
religious witness to the truth in the midst of lies has led
millions to feel that God has withdrawn from our world.

A young Native American in Louise Erdich's novel *Love
Medicine* expresses this absence when he complains,

> God's been going deaf. Since the Old Testament,
> God's been deafening up on us. I read, I see.
> Besides the dictionary, which I'm constantly in
> use of, I had this Bible once. I read it. I found
> there was discrepancies then and now. It
> struck me. Here God used to raineth bread
> from clouds, smite the Phillipines, sling fire
> down on red-light districts when people got
> stabbed. He even appeared in person every
> once in a while. God used to pay attention, is
> what I'm saying. ...Was there any sense relying
> on a God whose ears are stopped? Just like the
> government? I says then, right off, maybe we
> got nothing but ourselves (p. 194).

Such reflections come from persons fictional and real
who experience the horrors some psalms lament but not their
assurance that God hears and will assuage the suffering:

All day long my watchful foes persecute me;
countless are those who assail me.
Appear on high in my day of fear;
I put my trust in thee (Ps 56:2-3).

The scale of suffering in our time resists comprehension and induces numbing. We learned in grade school the specific tortures Nero visited on early Christians. Our childish nightmares replayed images of thousands of people like us flung to the lions, burned as human torches, branded with molten metal, sewn into skins of wild animals for dogs to tear at, tortured on the rack, body parts cut off one at a time to prolong the agony. Surely, we thought, Nero concocted the most ingenious torture methods ever. Now we know that Nero was Daffy Duck compared to Hitler, and every two-bit dictator in the world today out-Neroes Nero in techniques for inflicting pain. One wonders what purpose it serves even to name torturers who are as ubiquitous as they are vicious.

In Margaret Drabble's novel *The Gates of Ivory*, the character Stephen keeps a page of numbers for an "Atrocity Stories" booklet he is preparing. He notes that Rameses III killed 12,535 in his war with the Libyans and that Tamburlaine, who massacred 100,000 at a time, built towers of skulls in Syria. In the twentieth century, the numbers of victims soar:

800,000 Armenians
12 to 32 million: Belgian Congo
6 million Jews
3 million: Bangladesh
20 million: Soviet labor camps
2 million: Vietnam
1 to 2 million: Cambodia
28-80 million: the Chinese cultural revolution

A friend who reads Stephen's list asks if such numbers are not so bizarre as to fail as language. The novel's narrator wonders whether the story form can encompass the suffering implied.

The mismatch between narrative and subject is too great. Why impose the story line of individual fate upon a story which is at least in part to do with numbers? A queasiness, a moral scruple overcomes the writer at the prospect of selecting individuals from the mass of history, from the human soup. Why this one, why not another? Why pause here? Why discriminate? Why seek the comfort of the particular, the anguish of the particular? (Drabble, p. 138).

If the novelist worries about merely describing the pain, what is the burden of the Christian who seeks to know the role of God in it? Are all those persecuted in our time—with hunger, torture, war, displacement—persecuted with the Christ? Can we even call them persecuted subjects or must we name them random victims? Are they part of the "global crucifixion of Jesus," Archbishop Raymond Hunthausen's phrase for nuclear holocaust? After all, how many Jobs can live in the world at once? How many say with the Santo Domingo disk jockey, "And after life, for me remains the hope of death," or ask the question from liberation theology, "Is there life before death?" Do the victimized millions know that they suffer with Jesus, even know who Jesus is, or are they routinely ravaged as part of the Body of Christ, perhaps unaware of that body in which they live?

Maimonides says, "A Jew killed, not for resistance, but just because he is a Jew, is holy." The beatitude, "Blessed are they who suffer persecution for justice," makes the same claim for humankind. Persons violated or killed just because they live, or try to live, are holy because justice entitles them to the life they are born into. Though many who suffer in this post-Christian era, in numbers often unrecorded, suffer in a dark night where God cannot be seen, they can nonetheless name God in the bodies of their brothers and sisters, the Body of Christ. The prisoner who wrote, *"Dios no mata"* in blood on the walls of an Argentinian torture chamber was able to name a dimension of God in the absence of God: "God does not kill."

In *Lilac and Flag*, John Berger's final novel in a trilogy about the end of peasants in the modern world, the author has two men washed up on the shore of a mythical modern city say to each other:

> In history things often happen when nothing seems to be happening.
> Like some nights.
> Yes, history has nights and days, said Murat.
> And now it's night?
> Now it's night, it's been night for a long while (Berger, p. 60).

The character can see no end to the night. This century rehearses the story of Job a billion times over, and we hardly dare the temerity to claim that each tale is a tale of suffering with the suffering God, still the Light of the World in its darkest of nights. Although the scale of persecution is massive, and thus God suffers exponential pain, evidence indicates that the response remains individual, as particular as one death on a cross.

In an account of his internment at Buchenwald, Jacques Lusseyran categorizes the diverse persons interned there, the most transcendent actions often emanating from the least likely of them. He concludes that there are no models for living in our times, that only the saints and mystics can live well now. Etty Hillesum, a Dutch student and a Jew who worked to assist inmates in the German concentration camps, eventually died in one herself. In her letters from the Westerbork camp, she imagines all of Europe turning into one vast concentration camp, and she tries to draw meaning from the experience for others as well as herself.

She thinks that many in the camp don't give much occasion to love them and admonishes those prisoners who say, "We don't want to think, we don't want to feel, it's best to shut your eyes to all this misery." Suffering is part of human existence, she insists, and must be faced because "if we have nothing to offer a desolate post-war world but our bodies saved at any cost, if we fail to draw new meaning from the deep wells of our distress and despair, then it will not be enough." Neither Hillesum nor Lusseyran doubts that mass suffering is the suffering of individuals who, despite appearances, retain the capacity for human choice.

And yet, what blessing for the masses persecuted in our time? Indeed, God blesses not the masses but each person among them crucified by malnutrition, torture, or refugee status. Each one—defying logic and numbers—is more dear than the birds of the air and the lilies of the field. That is the promise of, "Blessed are they who suffer persecution for justice sake, for theirs is the kingdom of heaven." The persecuted are made poor, like those in the first beatitude, and thus they are made rich by receiving the kingdom. Every prop pulled from under them, they may finally lean on God alone. In response to the query, "Which master do you serve, God or mammon?" they answer resoundingly through their tears or through their silence, "God." Because they are not against God, they are with God. Though sometimes they may be tempted to curse God or the darkness that keeps them from seeing God.

They live like the isolated old man who sleeps on the floor beside the bed of his wife with Alzheimer's disease. Like the Brazilian street urchin who runs from the police and shines shoes to support his brothers and sisters. They are the people for whom hope is a state of mind, not much related to the state of the world. As Vaclav Havel says of hope, "Its deepest roots are in the transcendental." Those who suffer injustice, struggling to live the human life that justice demands, live the transcendental.

"Rejoice and be glad," says Jesus, "for your reward is great." "Be glad," from the Greek verb *agalliasthai*, means "to leap exceedingly." To leap for joy. Are you downtrodden? Jump up to the sky! Violated? Spring up and begin again! Ridiculed? Dance a jig around your tormentor! Leap as

David did when, victorious, he danced before the tabernacle of the King of Kings. Tales abound of early Christian martyrs going out with joyful shouts to face the lions. The disciples walking the road to Emmaus "with their faces full of gloom" just after the crucifixion, stymied by the empty tomb and a reported vision of angels, meet a stranger on the way. When they reach the village and press him to stay with them and he breaks bread with a blessing, they open their eyes beyond the gloom, recognize Jesus, and ask themselves, "Did we not feel our hearts on fire as he talked with us on the road?" (Lk 24:32). In the midst of despair, and with many trials ahead, they nonetheless know blessing in his presence, experience a taste of heaven.

When he calls his disciples, Jesus promises them an easy yoke and a light burden, not the absence of a yoke or burden. The word "yoke" is a cognate of the Sanskrit *yoga*, which in Hinduism stands for a number of means for liberation. Although literally meaning "to bind," *yoga* results in breaking the bonds between the spirit and the world. It implies mystical union with the divine as a consequence of liberation from the world, in Christian terms, the kingdom of heaven preferred to the realm of mammon. The yoke of Jesus binds us to him and thus helps break our other bonds. It is light because it is borne by two, Jesus and the one persecuted with him.

Bonhoeffer thinks the last beatitude is addressed directly to the disciples because only they can understand it. If suffering means being cut off from God, he says, one cannot really suffer while living in communion with God. "From the cross there comes the call, 'blessed, blessed.'" But the suffering is real, one may rejoin, for those who hang on the cross, whether or not they call out the name of God. Suffering—disruption, persecution—is part of life and brings blessing to the seeker after justice. Still, it is not liquidated by the blessing, by the ability to leap and be glad.

Martin Niemoller, a committed Christian and father of seven, went to a concentration camp for resisting Hitler.

When someone offered condolences to his aged parents, Niemoller's father responded that pity should be reserved for those who miss out on the joy of the cross. His parents felt that the worst Niemoller could have done was refuse to be the martyr God called him to be. Daniel Berrigan's mother showed similar convictions when an interviewer asked her if she realized her son was breaking the law. "Not God's law," she answered. In the eyes of those who knew them well, Niemoller and Berrigan suffered persecution for justice, and knew joy.

Etty Hillesum was a secular Jew, caught up in the bohemian pleasures of students and colleagues until she experienced the Holocaust. In *An Interrupted Life*, she thinks about the consequences of deportation:

> And the funny thing is that I don't feel I'm in their clutches anyway, whether I stay or am sent away. I find all that talk so cliche-ridden and naive and can't go along with it anymore. I don't feel in anybody's clutches; I feel safe in God's arms, to put it rhetorically, and no matter whether I'm sitting at this beloved old desk now or in a bare room in the Jewish district or perhaps in a labor camp under SS guards in a month's time—I shall always feel safe in God's arms. They may well succeed in breaking me physically, but no more than that. I may face deprivation and cruelty the likes of which I cannot imagine even in my wildest fantasies. Yet all this is as nothing compared to the immeasurable expanse of my faith in God and my inner receptiveness (Hillesum, p. 149).

Since she suffered persecution just because she was a Jew, as Maimonides said, Hillesum was holy. Furthermore, she learned to name God, and when she actually came to the camp she wrote to friends that she found the same basic materials of life there as elsewhere. She compares the sea gulls she can see from her bunk to "free thoughts in an open mind," and she walks along the barbed wire fence with a spring in her step. She practices *agalliasthai*, leaping for gladness.

I have known prisoners who deserved punishment for crime, but whose punishment wore on long beyond the time when it could have taught a lesson. In the end, it communicated only vengeance to the prisoners, who were persecuted. Often, prison conditions pile suffering on suffering, adding inhumane treatment to the isolation from society that prison was meant to be. I remember the radiant face of a prisoner who lived without privacy, decent food, or medical care. She told me she had refused to attend her mother's funeral because she would have had to go handcuffed to a guard. This despite the fact that she was neither dangerous nor likely to escape. She both wept and smiled as she said:

> In your first six months here you think of the people you hurt and are sorry. After that, it all seems like revenge. They want to destroy you, and they can make you bitter. But I refuse to be. I won't accept their conditions, and I won't let them punish my family by seeing me in chains. Instead, I'll stay here and say goodbye to my mother in my heart.

In her face and the face of other prisoners' I have seen the joy of the persecuted ones. They forego bitterness and spite, unlike the structures that contain them. They are among the blessed, the poor and forgotten who come into the kingdom even as they suffer. In the final beatitude, Jesus invites us all to do the same.

Conclusion

If you are poor in spirit,
    you have riches enough
      for today only.
The rest you gave away
    when you met compassion.
Still, you are rich in God,
    on whom you depend
    for tomorrow.
Your blessing is like Job's,
    you know God now
      not from the tales of others
      but from your own story.

When you mourn,
    you sense the world cannot go on for you
      as you have known it
      and expected it to be,
but your comfort lives beyond denial
    in a deeper pool of being.
You have crossed a threshold
    to rejoicing.

If you are meek,
    you can dare to be angry
      because God is in control
      and plots the appropriate targets.

You face off with them
> for the sake of the earth,
> > in which you delight as recompense.

If you hunger and thirst for justice,
> your longing does not allow you
> > to settle for half a loaf.

You are satisfied
> only as you bake the bread, eat God;

in the desert,
> you distinguish the mirage,
> keep walking toward real water, wine.

If you are merciful,
> you live in the Body that we all are,
> entangled with every creature
> > who shares its flesh and blood and spirit.

Since you know no "other,"
> you judge not and claim no dominion,
> but live in mercy,
> > unconstricted,
> > light in being.

You sing the song of community.

If you are pure in heart,
> you fly like an arrow
> and pray like a stream
> > coming near to the sea.

Every day you see
> God the ravishing,
> God the hopeful,
> God the suffering one
> > who walks at our side.

If you are a peacemaker,
> you move into breaches
> and bridge the high gaps,
> righting relationships,
> making straight the way.

As a "son of God,"
   you know who you are
   and laugh at the divine comedy
      of our connections.

If you suffer persecution for the justice
   you hunger after,
   you leap for joy at it,
      into the world's dark night.
You sense that the stars of heaven still shine,
   most visible to those
      with no lights of their own
      that break up the darkness.
You have become poor
   and, like the poor,
   have no jewels but stars
   —including the sun.

As a disciple, behold your program and your portrait. It is also the program and portrait of the one you follow, in his time and ours designed for the underdog, mapped out for the marginated. Of you who would follow the blessed one, who would not save but would spend your life, God asks the maximum but not the impossible. Though they need God's help for the living of them, the beatitudes are nonetheless practical, even necessary, if the world shall be saved. Accessible to all, yet uniquely phrased for Christians in the Sermon on the Mount, they are not diagrams drawn by someone who can't speak the language. They are images painted by the one who is beyond all language. They are not the theories of an idealist; they are the practicable and patient advice of a friend.

They paint a portrait as well of the Christian community, of any real community, the salt of the earth and the light of the world, not in some future time but in inevitable consequence of its manner of living here and now. Like karma, the beatitudes flow from experience: "As you sow, so shall you reap." Though their blessings are gift not deserts. As with all gifts, a giver is implied, stage front or in the wings, waiting for the smile while sending in the bouquets. Carl Vaught says in *The Sermon on the Mount* that the Greek future tense emphasizes not what will happen later but the absolutely necessary consequences that follow upon an antecedent condition. You do this, I do that. A gift given by a giver who has promises to keep.

A gift given to a beggar who lives on the promises, breathes them, drinks them in, eats them. They are real food and drink. There is no other meal. To whom shall we go when we are poor and hungry? And when we are completely empty, with what shall we be filled?

I start out in a drizzle.
At the lake
rain drops reverberate
like children leaping.
I consider turning back
but stow my steamed-up glasses
in a pocket
that also takes in water
and keep to the path.

Under trees whose leaves
weave awnings,
I convince myself one puzzle
piece of sky turns blue.
As water burns my eyes
and snakes into shirt and shoes,
my body hunches into itself,
desiring to live between drops.

The clouds crack like eggs
hatching giant water dragons.

Soon my sweater reeks
like the sodden dog who trots beside,

squinting accusations at me,
and jeans are limp ice papered to legs.
I can no longer deny I am wet.

But now the green of the surrounding prism,
red rays of sumac and autumn dogwood,
black crows commenting on the cosmos,
draw my face up.
I slow to a stroll,
saturated,
protect myself from nothing.

Perhaps on the way home
the great blue heron
will do its glissade over the lake.

References

Barclay, William. *The Gospel of Matthew*. Rev. ed. Vol. I. Philadelphia: The Westminster Press, 1975.

Berger, John. *Lilac and Flag: An Old Wives' Tale of a City*. New York: Pantheon, 1990.

Berrigan, Daniel and Thich Nhat Hahn. *The Raft Is Not the Shore: Conversations Toward a Buddhist/Christian Awareness*. Boston: Beacon, 1975.

Beston, Henry. *The Outermost House: A Year of Life on the Great Beach of Cape Cod*. New York: Penguin, 1976.

Camera, Helder. *The Desert Is Fertile*. Maryknoll, NY: Orbis Press, 1974.

Cardenal, Ernesto. *The Gospel in Solentiname*. 4 vols. Maryknoll, NY: Orbis Press, 1982.

Collins, Raymond. *Introduction to the New Testament*. Garden City, NY: Doubleday, 1983.

Dillard, Annie. *Holy the Firm*. New York: Harper and Row, 1977.

Drabble, Margaret. *The Gates of Ivory*. New York: Viking, 1991.

Eichenberg, Fritz. *Art and Faith*. Pendle Hill, 1953. Quoted in *The Catholic Worker*, Mar.-Apr. 1991, p. 4.

Eisley, Loren. *The Star Thrower.* New York: Times Books, 1978.

Erdich, Louise. *Love Medicine.* New York: Holt, 1984.

Ferguson, John. *War and Peace in the World's Religions.* New York: Oxford University Press, 1978.

Garrow, David J. *Bearing the Cross: Martin Luther King, Jr., and the Southern Christian Leadership Conference.* New York: Vintage, 1988.

Goodall, Jane. *Through a Window: My Thirty Years with the Chimpanzees of Gombe.* Boston: Houghton Mifflin, 1990. Quoted in "One of the Lucky Ones," *American Way,* Feb. 1, 1991, pp. 67 ff.

Hamm, M. Dennis, SJ. *The Beatitudes in Context: What Luke and Matthew Meant.* Wilmington, DE: Michael Glazier, 1990.

Havel, Václav. *Disturbing the Peace.* New York: Knopf, 1990.

Hillesum, Etty. *An Interrupted Life.* New York: Pantheon, 1983.

——————. *Etty Hillesum: Letters from Westerbork.* New York: Random House, 1986.

Leddy, Mary Jo. *Re-Weaving Religious Life: Beyond the Liberal Model.* Mystic, CT: Twenty-Third, 1990.

Lusseyran, Jacques. *And There Was Light.* New York: Parabola, 1987.

Macy, Joanna. *Despair and Personal Power in the Nuclear Age.* Philadelphia: New Society Publishers, 1983.

May, Rollo. *Power and Innocence.* Toronto: George McLeod, 1972.

Merchant, Carolyn. *The Death of Nature: Women, Ecology, and the Scientific Revolution.* San Francisco: Harper and Row, 1983.

Merton, Thomas. *The Asian Journal*. New York: New Directions, 1973.

O'Connor, Flannery. *The Complete Stories*. New York: Farrar, Straus, Giroux, 1972.

Ortega y Gasset, Jose. *The Revolt of the Masses*. Notre Dame, IN: University of Notre Dame Press, 1985.

Shlaes, Amity. *Germany: The Empire Within*. New York: Farrar, Straus, Giroux, 1991.

Smith, Huston. *The Religions of Man*. New York: Harper and Row, 1965.

Stern, Fritz. *Dreams and Delusions: The Drama of German History*. New York: Knopf, 1987.

Vanier, Jean. "A Vision of Community," *Pax Christi USA*, Winter 1991, pp. 20-21.

Vaught, Carl G. *The Sermon on the Mount*. Albany, NY: State University of New York Press, 1986.

Weil, Simone. *Gravity and Grace*. New York: G. P. Putnam's Sons, 1952.

_____ . *Simone Weil Reader*. New York: David McKay, 1977.

Wills, Gary. *Lincoln at Gettysburg: The Words That Remade America*. New York: Simon and Schuster, 1992.